DRAMA FICTION POETRY

THE FACILITY
& OTHER TEXTS RE-IMAGINING ANTIGONE

ACKNOWLEDGEMENTS

Edited by Barbara Bleiman, Andrew McCallum and Lucy Webster

Cover: © Alex Kirby

Published by the English & Media Centre, London, 2022

978 1 906101 70 1

Printed by Stephens and George

The Facility & Other Texts – Re-imagining Antigone **is part-funded by and published with the support of The Classical Association.**

CONTENTS

INTRODUCTION FOR TEACHERS

This anthology is in EMC's *Cultural Conversations* series. Each publication in the series brings together texts that relate to each other in some way, with interesting connections that demonstrate to students some key ideas about literature – for instance about traditions, genres and conventions, the way that writers draw on earlier work for inspiration, how audiences read texts over time in different ways, what makes some texts endure and the relationship between readers and writers.

The anthology is based on Sophocles' tragedy *Antigone*, a play that has resonated with countless audiences through the centuries, having been translated, adapted and re-envisioned numerous times, by different writers, for different contexts. Its exploration of power and coercion, conflicts between individual, family and political interests, resistance and rebellion, youth standing out against the older generation, religious beliefs and rites versus more secular exigencies, and what it means to be female in a male-controlled society, have all offered rich possibilities for translation to different political realities and societies. Among other adaptations, *Antigone* has been re-envisioned: as a play for occupied France in World War II, with a hidden message about resisting Nazi control; as a comment on apartheid South Africa; as a reflection on race and police violence against black people in the USA; as a novel about Islamic radicalisation and the state of the British nation, along with many more.

In the anthology you will find specially commissioned new writing based on *Antigone*: poems by Valerie Bloom, Inua Ellams; a short story by Phoebe Roy, a play by Sarah Hehir and a short story and poem by me. Each writer has written a specially commissioned work, inspired by Sophocles' play, supported by a grant from the Classical Association. They have also written short reflections, both exploring what they took from the original text and commenting on their own writing, to help students engage with the issues of the play alongside the new texts. Some of the texts can potentially be read as stand-alone works, in particular the play and the short stories, though we think that they will offer a lot more to students if, as a bare minimum, they know an outline of the original play. So we have included a short summary in the anthology. Some students may, of course, have already had the pleasure of reading and studying the whole of Sophocles' play in Drama, Classics or as part of the English curriculum. Equally, some teachers may choose to read the whole play as a prelude to reading the new works. Reading the new texts alongside each other obviously also offers rich potential for comparison of what different contemporary writers have made of the Sophocles play, in different styles and genres.

The playscript by Sarah Hehir is a brilliant one-hour play, with lots of different parts for the classroom. As a work in its own right, it is a major new drama text that we hope will fill a gap in classroom reading. Suitable for KS3 and above, it both raises important themes for discussion and debate and introduces students to some of the key elements in a playwright's repertoire – dialogue, monologue, a chorus, physical action, symbolism and recurring motifs.

We hope you enjoy the opportunity to bring a classic, ancient text into conversation with some new interpretations by contemporary writers. Visit EMC's website for information on how to get the free classroom resources to support the study of these texts as part of a long cultural conversation.

Barbara Bleiman

Please note: you may feel this anthology is most appropriate for Year 9 and above. The classical play with which the texts in this anthology are in conversation explores a number of challenging and sensitive issues, for example suicide and death. The writers have also focused on some of these issues. The short story 'Being Antigone' includes one expletive on page 88.

INTRODUCTION FOR STUDENTS

This anthology is based on *Antigone*, a play written by the ancient Greek dramatist Sophocles, around 441 BCE. It's a play that has struck a chord with many people, in many different countries over the centuries and it has been adapted for different contexts and for new audiences. For instance, a French playwright, Jean Anouilh, wrote a version of *Antigone* during World War II, when France was occupied by the Nazis. He kept the Greek setting so it wasn't obvious to the Germans that there was a hidden message about resisting Nazi control. That message came across loud and clear though to the French audiences who saw the play! It's also been adapted by South African playwright Athol Fugard as a comment on apartheid. He set his play on Robben Island, where Nelson Mandela was imprisoned for many years. More recently, in 2014 in Ferguson, Missouri, community leaders, teachers, youth workers and drama groups put on a production called *Antigone in Ferguson*, to mark and protest about the death of a young black man, Michael Brown, at the hands of the police. Novelists, including Kamila Shamsie and Ali Smith have also written versions of *Antigone*.

What makes this play so powerful that it's been adapted so often? Well, it deals with really big themes that can apply in different societies and cultures – powerful strict rulers and what happens to those who resist their laws, what it's like to be female in a world where men rule the roost, conflicts between individual, family and political interests, youth standing up to age, religion and beliefs about death, burial and the afterlife, and much more.

In this anthology you will find specially commissioned new writing, based on *Antigone*, by poets Valerie Bloom and Inua Ellams, short story writers, Phoebe Roy and myself, and playwright, Sarah Hehir. Each writer has written a new text (or in the case of Valerie Bloom and myself, two), inspired by Sophocles' play. They have also written short commentaries, to help you engage with the issues of the original play and think about what each writer has done to adapt it and why.

These are texts in conversation with each other and we hope that you'll have great conversations about them too. Maybe you'll also want to write your own version of *Antigone* when you've read some of the ones in this anthology? If you decide to do that, you'll be contributing to a long tradition and keeping it alive!

Barbara Bleiman

The Story of Antigone

The back story – Antigone's family

The back story to *Antigone*, a Greek play, is deeply troubling and packed with family drama.

The story starts with Oedipus, a figure from Greek myth and one-time king of Thebes, a city in Greece. At birth Oedipus became separated from his parents, Laius and Jocasta, King and Queen of Thebes. This meant he grew up with no knowledge of either of them, a situation with bizarre and horrifying consequences. First, Oedipus unwittingly killed Laius; second, he married Jocasta. Let's put that another way: he killed his own father and married his own mother.

Family Tree

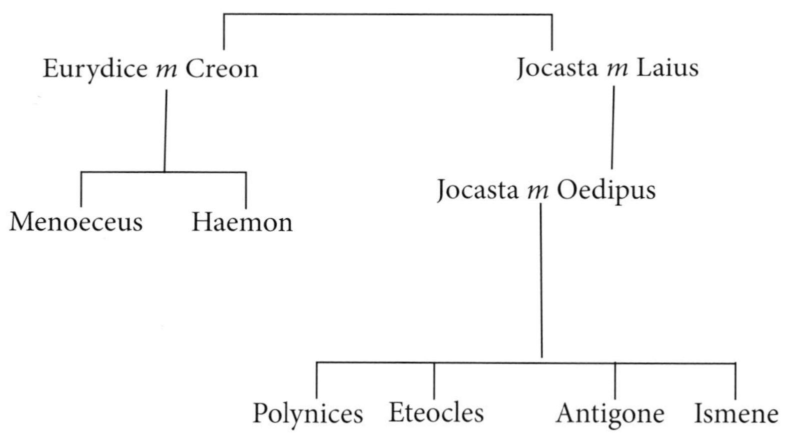

Oedipus and his mother, Jocasta, produced four children from their incestuous marriage: two boys, Polynices and Eteocles, and two girls, Antigone and Ismene. When Jocasta finally learned that she had married her own son, she was horrified and killed herself.

Oedipus was expelled from Thebes and his sons, Polynices and Eteocles, were put in charge instead. The plan was for them to take turns ruling the city. Each would hold power for a year before handing over control to the other. A good solution, you might think, but destined to end in tragedy thanks to a curse placed on the brothers by their father Oedipus, who was angry with his sons for allowing him to be disgraced and exiled as a beggar. Eteocles, the first to take charge, refused to hand over the throne at the end of his year. Polynices was so furious that his rightful turn at ruling had been denied to him that he formed an army and laid siege to Thebes. The Thebans fought hard, holding back Polynices' army. Finally, the two brothers decided on a face-off against each other. They met at the gates of the city and ended up killing each other.

The play starts – Creon refuses a burial for Polynices

At the start of Sophocles' play, Antigone's uncle (and Jocasta's brother), Creon, has taken over the throne of Thebes. Creon allows for Eteocles to be buried according to the expected rituals, with full honours.

But he views Polynices as a traitor for waging war on Thebes. He declares that Polynices should receive no honours, or even a burial at all. This means that Polynices is denied the right to one of the most important religious rituals of ancient Greek society. The gods themselves would expect it. Failing to bury him does not just dishonour Polynices and his family but also infuriates the gods, bringing certain trouble to the ruling family of Thebes and its people.

Antigone is determined to bury Polynices' body

Where do Oedipus' remaining children, Antigone and Ismene, stand on their Uncle Creon's decision? What do they think should be done? As two young girls, perhaps they should just stay silent as might be expected and obey Creon's orders. But this does not happen. Antigone refuses to obey Creon, and instead decides to bury the body of her brother herself. Twice, she visits Polynices' corpse, which is lying out on the open ground, where crows can pick at it. She cannot bury the body properly, so instead she gives Polynices a symbolic burial, scattering handfuls of earth over him. On a second visit to repeat this symbolic act, Antigone is caught by Creon's guards who forcibly take her away and drag her in front of Creon, telling him how she has been disobeying his decree.

Antigone is resolute, despite her sister Ismene's pleas

Creon is furious and insists that she must give up her attempts to bury her brother. She is just a young girl but rather than caving in, she stands up to him, refusing to apologise or change her mind. She tells him that if he releases her, she will go straight back to Polynices' corpse and once again try to give him a symbolic burial. Creon's anger increases but she resists his threats and his fury. Her sister Ismene is afraid for her, and intimidated by Creon. She pleads with Antigone to obey their uncle, but Antigone won't back down. Creon is equally uncompromising. Though Antigone is his niece, and is also engaged to be married to his own son, Haemon, he won't change his mind, or show leniency. She must obey him, or face the consequences.

Haemon appeals to his father; Creon shuts Antigone in a cave to die

Haemon pleads desperately with his father on behalf of Antigone but he gets nowhere – Creon remains unmoved. It's a stalemate – Creon and Antigone are both quite determined not to budge. In the end, Creon orders that Antigone should be shut up inside a cave and left there until she dies of starvation. The entrance to the cave is covered with a large stone. Antigone's fate looks sealed.

The prophet Tiresias warns Creon to change his mind

Creon has made his decision; he has acted as a firm and determined ruler who won't stand for any rebellion or resistance. But soon after he has ordered that Antigone be shut in the cave, he receives a visit from Tiresias, an old blind prophet, who is able to predict the future. He warns Creon of dreadful omens from the gods, who have been angered by his actions. He urges Creon to reconsider his decision on the burial of Polynices and the incarceration of Antigone. His words hit home hard. Finally, Creon realises that he's made a terrible mistake and hurries to bury the body of Polynices, before going on to the cave to free Antigone.

Too late! Only Creon and Ismene survive

He is too late! By the time the cave door is opened Antigone has hung herself with her own garments. Haemon, who had been waiting by the cave entrance, so that he could be reunited with Antigone, is beside himself with grief, and kills himself with his sword, in front of his father. To make things even worse, Creon's wife Eurydice also commits suicide, when news is brought to her at the palace that Haemon, her son, is dead.

Only now does Creon realise what he has done. By his actions, he has brought about the deaths, not only of his niece, Antigone, but also his own wife and son. Ismene lives on, the only survivor out of the four siblings. Oedipus and Jocasta's children, it seems, have been punished terribly for the historic wrongs springing from their parents' incestuous marriage.

The Facility

A play by Sarah Hehir

I raise up my voice, not so that I can shout, but so that those without a voice can be heard.

Malala Yousafzai

Let not any one pacify his conscience by the delusion that he can do no harm if he takes no part, and forms no opinion. Bad men need nothing more to compass their ends, than that good men should look on and do nothing.

John Stuart Mill

The setting:

The Facility – a detention centre for young miscreants. The time is an indeterminate future in an undefined land, The Realm, where citizens are ruled by The Society: a rich and powerful political elite.

Characters:

ANTIGONE	A miscreant
ISMENE	A miscreant, mother and Antigone's sister
POLYNICE*	A miscreant who speaks from beyond the grave
CREON	Prison governor and Haemon's father
HAEMON	Head of Education. Creon's son
GUARD 1	
GUARD 2	
MISCREANTS	Young inmates of The Facility
CROW	Creon's conscience
CHORUS	The community, faith leaders, animals, media, citizens, bureaucracy, the voice of reason, dancing men

A note on the staging:

When staging the play, you may decide that the characters and chorus remain on stage at all times and the focus is shifted through lighting or action.

* In Sophocles' play, the character was a man called Polynices. Here Polynice is female.

Prologue

ANTIGONE	Ismene listen. Wake up! They aren't telling us anything.
ISMENE	They told us that Polynice is dead.
ANTIGONE	But that's not enough. What about the how and why and when and where she died?
ISMENE	In her cell. Last night.
ANTIGONE	But how and why?
ISMENE	Shush. A guard is coming.
GUARD 2	(*SHOUTS*) Lockdown.
ANTIGONE	(*SHOUTS*) Oy! You have to let us out.
GUARD 2	Not today. Exercise is cancelled.
GUARD 1	Education is cancelled.
ANTIGONE	(*SHOUTS*) Let us out. Our friend is dead.
GUARD 2	Food will be brought to you. Work will be posted under your doors.
ISMENE	Please let us out. We need to talk about Polynice. We need to remember her.
GUARD 1	We should give them time to grieve together.
GUARD 2	(*SHOUTS*) Lockdown.

ANTIGONE (*SHOUTS*) What happened to Polynice?

GUARD 2 (*SHOUTS*) Lockdown.

ANTIGONE (*SHOUTS*) You have to tell us!

GUARD 2 (*SHOUTS*) Lockdown.

~

CHORUS A tragedy
An unfortunate incident
Ill-fated
Unavoidable
Incomprehensible

~

ANTIGONE You give us no explanation. You take no blame. You say no sorry.

GUARD 2 Polynice. Outsider.

GUARD 1 Polynice. Good at chess. Better than me.

GUARD 2 Lockdown.

~

CHORUS Taunts and prods and pokes
Graffiti scrawled across her wall
A rat, dead in her bed
Go home, whispered through her door

~

ANTIGONE Ismene! We have to do something. Creon will take the death of Polynice and wrap it up in administration, layer after layer, like chips in paper.

~

CHORUS Polynice

Disposable

Forgettable

Flotsam

Jetsam

Lagan

Derelict

Arrived in a ship

Barely a boat

Hardly afloat

A dinghy

Alone

Already sinking

~

ANTIGONE Creon will bury the truth along with her body. Our questions will forever be words rattling around our cells: rubbed smooth like seaglass until there are no sharp edges left to lash out with.

ISMENE Your anger isn't helping. We need to grieve.

ANTIGONE We need to scream.

ISMENE We need to speak her name with dignity.

ANTIGONE What is dignity when you die alone in The Facility?

ISMENE Dignity is speaking the truth about who she was:
she won at Chess with her back turned
tied chewy purple snakes into knots with her tongue
shared her shower gel with anyone and everyone
recited poems by dead white men from long ago and far away.

ANTIGONE 'Darkling I listen'.

~

POLYNICE 'Darkling I listen; and, for many a time
I have been half in love with easeful Death.'

~

ISMENE Sung the Song of Solomon to rise above the rowdy night.

* From 'Ode to a Nightingale' by John Keats

ANTIGONE 'Set me as an amulet upon thine arm and upon they heart –'*

~

POLYNICE 'For love is as strong as death.'*

~

ISMENE She used the kettle to cook eggs stolen from the kitchen. She drew a picture of my baby girl to give me on my birthday.

ANTIGONE And wrote a poem to push under my door when I thought I couldn't take any more of this.

~

POLYNICE We pawns move forward in formation

To fight one step at a time, without ever turning back

~

ANTIGONE We will fight for your name to be spoken Polynice. We will shout until your story is told. We will not be silenced. (*SHOUTS*) We will not be silent. Rise up with me Ismene.

GUARD 2 Governor Creon forbids it!

ANTIGONE Let the death of Polynice fill these cells with rage!

* Adapated from a translation of the 'Song of Solomon' or 'Song of Songs'

ISMENE	We don't need more rage. We need a quiet time to remember her. We need to gather and hold hands, to sit and share our stories and sing our songs. We need to cry.
ANTIGONE	Rise up!
GUARD 1	Quiet. Please.
GUARD 2	Governor Creon will not tolerate disobedience.
ANTIGONE	Rise up!
GUARD 1	You'll get a mark against your name. Loss of privileges. Loss of exercise time.
ANTIGONE	Bring it on!
GUARD 1	Trouble will mean no screens for weeks. No library. No contact.
ANTIGONE	You think we care about any of that?
ISMENE	Be careful, Antigone. They can stop our visits. They can do what they want.
	HAEMON enters.
HAEMON	I've brought you the regulation worksheets to fill out: verbs and adverbs and other useless stuff. And when you've finished them, you can write an ode to Polynice.

ISMENE	Like to a nightingale.
ANTIGONE	What happened to Polynice, sir? What happened in her cell last night?
HAEMON	I have been told it was a tragedy.
ANTIGONE	A tragedy? Yes! But not an accident.
HAEMON	Polynice was a good student. The best.
ANTIGONE	You don't believe someone can die alone in their cell by accident!
HAEMON	I can't comment. There will be an enquiry.
ANTIGONE	Was she being bullied? Harassed? Hassled? Manhandled?
HAEMON	We all know Polynice lived through troubled times long before she arrived at The Facility. Long before she arrived in The Realm. I wrote up all of her history in my report.
ANTIGONE	Report for what?
HAEMON	To support her sanctuary claim. But it wasn't enough. Her application was turned down last night.
ANTIGONE	You denied her sanctuary.
HAEMON	Not me. Not us. We tried. But Creon said her case to stay in The Realm was weak.

ANTIGONE Then Creon will pay for this!

HAEMON I understand the agony you feel but lashing out won't bring Polynice back.

ISMENE steps forward.

ISMENE Sir, we don't want to cause trouble but we don't want to share our sadness through locked cell doors. We want to be together to remember her.

HAEMON I'll speak to Governor Creon but I can't promise he'll grant your request.

CROW lands on CREON'S window.

CREON Not now Crow. It's not a good time. Can't you see that there's trouble in paradise?

CROW How cruel to ask a blind crow what he can see.

CREON Your eyes see more than mortals.

CROW I can hear well enough and what I hear is that some of my soul's poetry is rubbing off on you Creon. Be careful, flesh of my flesh, or you may start listening to your conscience.

CREON	I listen. I have listened. Just not right now. I'm busy. I fear there's trouble brewing.

CROW	I can never understand why you humans spend so much of your time in needless strife.

CREON	And what? You crows live and let live?

CROW	I'm not the one on trial here.

CREON	And neither am I!

CROW	No. But. A. Girl. Did. Die.

Parodos*

CHORUS Someone's dead

Someone died

When?

Last night?

Of what? Old age? Pestilence? The plague?

No. An untimely death. Young.

As young as me?

Younger.

A child?

A teenager.

What a horror show. What sorrow.

Death by misadventure? By disease? By mistake?

All untimely deaths are tragedies.

Let their spirit wings grow.

There is no death, only a change of lands.

So lose not heart or despair.

Whosoever has come, shall depart.
All shall have their turn.

But how did they die? Tell me so
I can better protect my daughter:
better protect my son.

I heard it was a beautiful girl with a lovely smile. Knocked down by a car. Drunk driver. Hit and run.

* First song sung by the chorus in a Greek tragedy

No!

I heard it was a strong boy with
a straight back and a sharp mind.
Cancer. A brain tumour. Struck down
in his prime.

No!

I heard it was one of the kids from
The Facility. Locked up on the hill.

A miscreant?

Murdered by another inmate?

An overdose?

Suicide?

A knife attack?

Not only a miscreant but an
outsider.

Oh?

An unaccompanied refugee looking
for sanctuary.

I see.

Freeloading Felon Found Dead In
Cell.

Sudden Death of Immigrant Infidel.

First Episode

HAEMON enters with a box of musical instruments.

HAEMON Guard 2: unlock the cells. Let the children out. My father, Governor Creon, has decreed that they may have a short service in memory of Polynice.

GUARD 2 First log the tools.

HAEMON These aren't tools. They are instruments for making music, not weapons of war.

GUARD 2 Anything in the hands of a miscreant is considered a weapon.

~

POLYNICE Even words

~

HAEMON Fine. I've logged the maracas and clackers and rainsticks. Now unlock the cells. Please.

GUARD 2 lets the MISCREANTS out including ANTIGONE and ISMENE

ISMENE Thank you. Can we hold hands?

GUARD 2 No. No touching.

HAEMON Yes. You can hold hands.

ISMENE We gather together.

MISCREANTS We gather together.

~

CHORUS From different bands

Backgrounds

Beliefs

From different lands

We gather together to remember Polynice

~

HAEMON A young poet. A talented writer. A good student.

GUARD 1 Funny. She often made me laugh after a long night shift.

ISMENE She was our friend who came to this land.

~

CHORUS Fleeing war

No mum or dad left to mourn her

Landing on unfriendly beaches to find no family

No warm welcome

No easy ride

Only the open arms of villains and

delinquents

Exploitation

Castigation

Rejection

⁀

ISMENE She had no food. No home. No clothes except the ones she stood in. She got in with a bad crowd. What else could she do?

ANTIGONE takes off her trainers and ties the laces together.

MISCREANTS Say her name.

HAEMON Polynice. The girl who could turn grammar into beauty like Rumpelstiltskin spinning gold.

MISCREANTS Like Rumpelstiltskin spinning gold.

ANTIGONE swings her trainers wildly above her head.

ANTIGONE What puke and waffle. What toxic barf, spewed like maximus vomitus upon us as if we're mewling kittens or white mice, still pinkskinned. Open your eyes! Creon didn't protect Polynice and he won't protect any of us. And now nothing will be done. Nothing will be said.

ISMENE Antigone, sit down.

ANTIGONE No! I won't sit down. It's you, Ismene, who should stand up. Stand up with me! Stand up and shout so none of us are buried in Creon's silence.

ISMENE Creon will punish us for protesting.

ANTIGONE Creon can do what he likes. Believe me, his guilt in this will hang like a leaden chain around his neck. Last night, Creon told Polynice she would be transported back to the land she fled from. Can he claim ignorance of this cruelty?

~

CHORUS What could one man do to stop it?

~

ANTIGONE Forgive me, Ismene, for not feeling grateful that Creon allows us a moment to mourn. Pardon me for not getting down on my knees and thanking our overlord for small mercies. (*BANGS THE DRUM*) Wake up! Creon gives us crumbs while he eats cake.

ISMENE This service isn't for you, Antigone. It's for Polynice. Sit, so we can sing our songs and share our memories.

ANTIGONE Sit and sing? Really sister? This is not the time for lullabies.

ANTIGONE hands out instruments to the MISCREANTS.

Creon cares nothing for us. Enough is enough.

ISMENE We are in no position to fight Creon, so why try?

ANTIGONE Because not trying means we have given up.

~

CHORUS Complicit

~

ANTIGONE My eyes are now open.

ISMENE You look dangerous Antigone.

ANTIGONE Dangerous is good! Commit yourself Ismene and fight for change.

ISMENE How, when we are powerless?

ANTIGONE Alone, we are powerless. But together we can make a noise that is deafening.

ISMENE Our protests will never be heard. It is our memories of Polynice that will keep her alive.

ANTIGONE What good are memories if they aren't to spark a light to ignite a fire? We are crushed beneath Creon's power; our fire has to be nuclear if we stand a chance of destroying it. Apocalyptic. We have to smash The Facility from its foundations: blast his command to smithereens. Will you help me Ismene?

ISMENE Have you forgotten what will happen if we step out of line?

~

POLYNICE Us pawns move forward in formation
To fight one step at a time, without ever turning back

~

CHORUS A pawn's role: to protect the king.

~

ISMENE You expect me to fight against Governor Creon? My family has nothing. I was born into nothing like my mother and her mother before her. I'll die with nothing. But if I'm lucky, I'll get out of The Facility some day and bring up my daughter to hope for more.

ANTIGONE Hope! What use is that without action? Without anger?

ISMENE Can't you see, Antigone, that your anger is pointless? Creon and his kind will never listen to miscreants like us.

ANTIGONE I'd rather die fighting than whimper away because Creon's power decrees it.

ISMENE There are different kinds of power Antigone.

ANTIGONE Don't talk to me Ismene. You have chosen your side.

ANTIGONE bangs the drum and encourages the MISCREANTS to do the same.

GUARD 2 Enough! Lock them up.

GUARD 2 swoops in and wrestles the instruments from the MISCREANTS and locks them up.

First Stasimon*

'Ode to Man': a simple song sung by the CHORUS with great passion and accompanying dance moves.

CHORUS We are men
Born to be men
The Y chromosome is so strong
We are leaders
Born to be leaders
We have testosterone
Testosterone!
Testosterone!
It's a chemical surge we have!
Power and war
More and more
It's an urge we won't suppress.
Manhood makes us
Stronger and slicker
Superior
Brainier
Better and bigger
Logical decision makers
Record breakers
Victim haters
Brave, brave, brave

* A choral ode between episodes in a Greek tragedy

It's biological

We're mythological

It's biological

We're allegorical

We're men

We're men

We're men!

~

HAEMON enters and turns off the music. GUARD 1 carries the speakers away.

Second Episode

CREON	I should never have listened to you Haemon.
HAEMON	They're upset. Emotions are running high.
CREON	That's why they need to be contained! Their immature ideals quickly twist into dangerous uprisings.
HAEMON	Their friend is dead.
CREON	And when allowed to mourn, they lost control. They are only ever one step away from turning into a radicalised mob: a hint of an injustice and the vacuum of their adolescent brains ignites with rage.
HAEMON	But what if they're right? Did Polynice decide that death was preferable to being sent back to a land that would torture and kill her? We claim to take rebels from other lands. The System claims to shelter them.
CREON	The System, not me, decides who gets sanctuary. Her fate was out of my control.
HAEMON	Was it?
CREON	Of course! They can't accept every disgruntled outsider. Surely even

you, Haemon, are not so naïve as to think I have the power to change the fate of one sanctuary seeker? Am I listened to? You think I have the ear of The Legislators or The Leaders! No!

HAEMON I wrote a glowing report as her teacher. Guard 1, her personal officer, wrote a lengthy account outlining her excellent attitude and behaviour. Our words should have had an impact. Our words should have meant something.

CREON And I, too, did what I could. I ticked the boxes. I followed procedure.

HAEMON But if Polynice had been your son or daughter, would you have tried harder?

CREON I followed procedure.

HAEMON Did you father? Because I imagine supporting the sanctuary claim of a miscreant will never be a promotion winner: never see you rise through the ranks.

CREON No more talk.

HAEMON We could all have done more. My report could have been longer. I could have attached the poems Polynice wrote. Did you include her behaviour record and the courses she completed? The clubs she joined here?

CREON I followed procedure.

HAEMON Did you highlight her medical records that told the story of where she had come from, what she'd endured and what she'd return to?

CREON No more talk!

HAEMON Sanctuary should have been granted.

CREON No more talk of sanctuary. No more talk at all.

GUARD 2 Lockdown. Lockdown.

ANTIGONE To see injustice and keep silent is to be part of the problem.

~

CHORUS To see injustice and keep silent is to be complicit

~

ISMENE Take care Antigone.

Second Stasimon

CHORUS Antigone

Born into poverty

Crawled into ignorance

Tottered and toddled into nothing for breakfast

Effed and blinded her way through the doors of reception

Grew in confidence, singing and playing

Until told to sit down

And labelled a nuisance

Troublemaker

Idiot

Just like her father.

When the world won't behave

And there's no one to help you

You go off the rails

You seek out disruption

You rage and you fail

And you learn that life deals you

Unequal cards

And that someone is cheating

~

Third Episode

ISMENE If we speak now, we'll be thrown into isolation.

ANTIGONE I have a right to speak.

ISMENE Who gives you that right? Not Creon. Not The System.

ANTIGONE Ismene – if you're not with me then you're against me.

ISMENE I want to be with you but I can't afford to get marks against my name. Not now. I need to work towards release. I'm a mum, Antigone: stronger than ever and never before so weak. Now that I have a daughter, I am nothing without her.

ANTIGONE makes noise with whatever she can.

ANTIGONE Where is Polynice? Where will you bury her body? Where will you bury her story? Behind what will you hide this miscarriage of justice?

~

CHORUS Trouble and tragedy.

Fate and fortune.

~

ANTIGONE Why was Polynice worth so little to you, Creon?

~

CHORUS Apathy. Apathy. Dangerous apathy.

~

ANTIGONE Creon, you can't force me to be silent!

ISMENE Antigone, please.

ANTIGONE Shout for the downtrodden, the lost, the forgotten, the displaced, the exploited, the used and misused.

The MISCREANTS stamp their feet.

ANTIGONE Shout for Polynice, the oppressed, the neglected. Shout for your brothers and sisters, your sons and your daughters. Tell Creon we're done with his cowardly lies.

MISCREANTS Creon, we're done with your cowardly lies.

ISMENE watches, wary.

GUARD 2 No talking. No shouting. No spitting. No cursing.

ANTIGONE Say her name!

MISCREANTS Polynice.

ANTIGONE Say her name.

MISCREANTS Polynice. Polynice. Polynice.

The chant continues.

GUARD 2 Creon.

CREON What is it?

GUARD 2 It's the girl. The troublemaker.

CREON Antigone.

GUARD 2 She continues to protest. She shouts 'Polynice' until the chant is echoed up and down the landings.

CREON Aren't they all confined to their cells? Didn't I ban them from speaking that name?

GUARD 2 You did sir. But still she finds ways. She clicks her fingers and they stamp their feet.

CREON If they stamp their feet then take their trainers.

GUARD 2 Take their trainers and they dance in their socks.

CREON Then command her to lie still and silent on her bed.

GUARD 2 But how to enforce it? Whatever we do, she finds a way round it. Just when we think we've overpowered her, the stench of her protest reaches our noses. She smears the walls of her cells with words like:

GUARD 1 truth

GUARD 2 and

GUARD 1 guilt

GUARD 2 and

GUARD 1 lies.

CREON This must stop! Is not my word final? Have I no authority that a youth, a reprobate, a silly little girl thinks she can get the better of me? One more whisper and I will cast her into isolation. I will increase her sentence. I will not have this insurrection!

HAEMON What are you really suggesting father? We lock them all up and never let them out? Most of our miscreants are just lonely lost kids.

CREON They're criminals: here to be punished. Don't let them crawl in under your skin.

HAEMON The name Polynice has become for them a howl of rage against us.

CREON Polynice is no martyr. Her claim to stay in The Realm was found wanting by The System. I will not shoulder the blame for that.

HAEMON To not oppose is to enable. Polynice should have been granted sanctuary. Let's step out into the light father and stand together to voice our concerns.

CREON Son, I worry for you. What land do you think we're living in?

HAEMON The System is broken but no decree says it can never be mended. We must make a noise and get ourselves noticed. At every level, there will be those who think like us.

~

CHORUS Guards

Teachers

Rulers

Leaders

Legislators

~

HAEMON Let's put our hands up and say we've failed the miscreants here. We're failing them from long before they are dragged through our doors.

CREON My hopeless, helpless son.

HAEMON It doesn't have to be like this. We need a revolution in thinking. Let's stand up and be counted.

CREON My poor trusting child. This you must understand: we work in the shadows. Here, right here, we work in the dark corners of The Realm where no-one with power ever wants to be.

HAEMON But if we give the powerful a chance to stand in our shoes, they might finally legislate for change.

CREON They won't because they couldn't care less.

HAEMON Antigone isn't afraid to demand change.

CREON That's why we must crush her protests Haemon. Silence the memorials. Control the miscreants. Keep what happened here to the officials, the forms, the administration.

HAEMON Did you hear me father? Antigone isn't afraid.

CREON Guard 2! Bring me the girl who turns prayers into protest. Bring me this girl who smears faeces over the walls of the cell where she sleeps. Even animals don't live like that. Bring me the girl born into a cursed family: stupid enough to follow the path of crime that was, generation after generation, laid out before her. Bring me this girl who isn't afraid.

GUARD 2 (*SHOUTS*) Bring Antigone

HAEMON Why blame her? Why hate her? We have a common enemy. We can go against the grain, swim against the tide, stand together, unite. Please father.

CREON Bring me the girl.

HAEMON Spare her. She is not the problem. She's angry because she's principled and in pain: a brave young woman.

CREON And I am the man in charge!

CROW enters.

CREON I know, when you look at me, that you think the worst of me but I'm not a bad man.

CROW says nothing.

CREON Keeping these wild miscreants from harm is my daily miracle. That's what I do here. I'm a good man. Crow?

CROW says nothing.

CREON — If I let down my guard, if I admit to making a mistake, The System will shame me and discard me. In a sleight of hand, they will make me carry the burden of all of their crimes. Nothing to see here citizens, just a foolish old man.

CROW exits.

GUARD 2 — Bring Antigone.

ANTIGONE is brought forward.

GUARD 1 — Antigone. I have my orders from Creon.

HAEMON — Let me speak to her first.

GUARD 1 — Creon is expecting her.

HAEMON — Please.

GUARD 1 — One minute and no more. I, too, have a family to feed.

ANTIGONE — Creon has called for me and I am ready.

HAEMON — I think a simple apology will help appease Creon. Then, in our lessons, we will compose a list of what could be done to improve conditions here.

ISMENE	We will start small and gain momentum. A manifesto of miscreants: the lost and forgotten. If we're respectful and careful, we'll make an impression.
ANTIGONE	I pity you both. Your misplaced hope is more dangerous than ignorance. I will speak my mind to Creon.
ANTIGONE	He's angry. He won't listen to you.
ANTIGONE	I'll make him listen.
HAEMON	He'll throw you into isolation.
ANTIGONE	He can stick my head on a stake for all I care.
HAEMON	Antigone, if you confront him, he will not be merciful.
ANTIGONE	No-one with even a pinch of power has ever been merciful to me. I won't be silenced. Your insipid protests, scribbled on paper, won't work! You will never be heard.

~

CHORUS

Imploring

Pleading

Beseeching

Begging

Down on your knees in supplication

Will you gobble the hopeful scraps

that he throws you?
Your polite lists
and well-meaning voices
are ants on a monolith
tickling the surface

~

ANTIGONE Creon uses our fear to rule us. It's not lists and requests that will change him. It's rage he understands. And I am raging!

ISMENE Please Antigone, wait until we're released and we'll make a plan. I'll strap my baby to my back and paint slogans on signs. I'll march through The Realm with you, arm in arm. But believe me when I say that, in here, we're powerless. Being young is against us anyway. And being women. Are you willing to risk the chance of freedom to bang our heads against a brick wall?

ANTIGONE Yes! If the alternative is doing nothing. I am going to blow the whistle so hard in Creon's ear that he will never get rid of the sound.

CHORUS How to blow the whistle?

ANTIGONE Ismene, we have a choice to speak up or to cower in the corner. Creon wants us to be selfish. He wants us to stay in our cells and look out for ourselves. That's how he controls us. But we have a common enemy. We must unite against Creon. Listen Ismene. I will howl for change. Polynice will not die in vain.

Third Stasimon

CHORUS

The state of The Realm is:

The CHORUS divides to debate the state of The Realm; the voices become increasingly disjointed and manic.

One citizen, one vote	The System never changes
You're alright Jill	don't rock the boat Jack
Strong and united	never more divided
	rich, richer, richest,
	survival of the fittest
Hail to our citizens	head below the parapet
Hope is our opiate	hope getting hopeless
Don't rock the boat Jack	
If you're fine Jack	
	are you alright Jack?
Accept	object
Zone out	stand up
Give up	protest
	shout out
Shut up	

The voices on both sides descend into animals squabbling: birds cawing, cats shrieking, dogs barking, wolves howling.

Fourth Episode

Throughout the scene there are intermittent rising and falling chants from the MISCREANTS.

MISCREANTS Revolt, revolt, rise up!

ANTIGONE Unlock the cells!

GUARD 2 Creon demands silence.

MISCREANTS Start the uprising! Hear our voices!

GUARD 1 Unlock the cells!

~

CHORUS The line between miscreant and guard is thin

Puppets dance on fraying strings

All inside

Marginalised

No hope of seeing the sun

~

MISCREANTS Unlock the cells!

HAEMON Antigone! Creon demands silence.

ANTIGONE The citizens deserve to know the truth and the truth is that a child died because Creon didn't save her.

HAEMON That isn't the truth. The battle is bigger than the forces inside The Facility. Creon's hands were tied.

ANTIGONE Don't make excuses for him. Polynice made it to our land and he didn't protect her. Last night, Creon destroyed any hope she had.

MISCREANTS Rise up!

HAEMON I understand that the news would have been a blow to her.

ANTIGONE A blow! It was the nail in her coffin.

MISCREANTS Polynice!

ANTIGONE Creon has called for me and I am ready.

GUARD 2 unlocks the cell. ANTIGONE is escorted to CREON by GUARD 1 and HAEMON.

HAEMON I bring to you Antigone. Friend of Polynice.

CREON Isolate her.

HAEMON Father, please listen. She's looking for a legacy.

CREON She's inciting revolution.

HAEMON Maybe an apology.

CREON Silence her.

HAEMON A promise to stand together. To try and do better.

ANTIGONE Tell me the truth Creon. Admit it. In your eyes, one life is worth less than another.

CREON How dare you assume what a life means to me?

ANTIGONE Admit you did nothing to protect Polynice.

CREON Insolent girl!

ANTIGONE You'd have fought tooth and nail to save your own child. But a miscreant, an outsider ... never! Admit it! You told Polynice she was going back to the bear pit – back to the beasts who drove her out of her land. Sanctuary was rejected and you accepted it. You handed Polynice the decree that killed her.

CREON Enough!

ANTIGONE Then, when Polynice was found dead, you hoped she would sink unnoticed: labelled her as an illegal sanctuary seeker, a convicted miscreant, a hopeless outsider ... who would miss her?

CREON I filled out the forms. I followed procedure.

ANTIGONE	And what did you write there? Did you draw a map to the inside of her heart and sketch in the scars?
CREON	Don't you dare question me.
ANTIGONE	Tell me the truth!
CREON	Guards! Lock her up!
ANTIGONE	(*TO GUARD 2*) Who was Polynice?
GUARD 2	Quiet. No trouble.
ANTIGONE	(*TO HAEMON*) Who was Polynice?
HAEMON	A welcome addition to our strange little classroom.
ANTIGONE	(*TO GUARD 1*) Who was Polynice?
GUARD 1	Funny. Polite. The only miscreant to wish me goodnight.
CREON	Guards! I said lock her up. Take her away. Take her to isolation. Take her shoes. Put her on suicide watch. I will not have a girl sink me deeper into this swamp. If you want to blame anyone, girl, blame yourself for being born into a family that could never do more than drag you up.
HAEMON	Father, stop.
CREON	Gutter girl! Scum, trash, garbage, junk.

HAEMON Stop!

CREON She believes my heart is rotten. She blames me for this. All of this. All of it. And who is she but a shrieking, hysterical girl, too stupid to see there might be a life outside these prison walls? (TO ANTIGONE) Do you even care about Polynice? Or is she just an excuse to shout? (TO HAEMON) Antigone's fight is for herself. She's as selfish as every other citizen in this land.

ANTIGONE Puppet!

CREON Antigone, you are no better than me.

ANTIGONE spits at Creon's feet.

HAEMON Father. Let her go back to her cell. Let her return to her friend Ismene. Let us find a new way to work through these troubled times – with courage and integrity.

Fourth Stasimon

CROW speaks to the CHORUS.

CROW You hold those committed by The System in this safe, decent and healthy facility.

~

CHORUS Inside the prison

tempers are rising

blood is boiling

miscreants bellowing

~

CROW You provide constructive regimes which address the offence and promote law-abiding behaviour whilst in The Facility and upon release into the lands beyond.

~

CHORUS Ask me no questions

I'll tell you no lies

~

CROW You deal fairly, openly and humanely with miscreants, regardless of their birth status or what land they hail from.

CHORUS Lock them up!

Lock them up!

~

CROW You promote equality of opportunity for all and combat discrimination wherever is occurs.

CREON Of course, of course.

~

CHORUS Let them out

Let them out

~

CROW You treat all miscreants with decency and respect.

CREON Can we stop this now? I have work to do.

Fifth Episode

From isolation, ANTIGONE continues to protest.

~

CHORUS Alone.

~

ANTIGONE Shout it out.

MISCREANTS Shout it out.

~

CHORUS Like many girls before her who stand up and speak out ...

~

ANTIGONE Unfair, unequal, buried, silenced.

MISCREANTS Unfair, unequal, buried, silenced.

~

CHORUS ... she risks being shot down.

~

ANTIGONE Say her name.

MISCREANTS Polynice.

~

CHORUS Head above the parapet.

~

ANTIGONE Shout it out!

MISCREANTS Freedom.

~

CHORUS Sacrifice.

Endurance.

~

ANTIGONE Shout it out!

MISCREANTS Injustice!

~

CHORUS Tainted. Troubled. Marked out.

No man will want to marry her now.

~

ISMENE When my baby was born, I was so tired, I didn't want to see her. I didn't choose to have her. I didn't think I could love her. But a midwife placed a cool pillow behind my head and helped me hold her. She wouldn't feed straight away. She wasn't sure what to do and refused to let me or the midwife help her. She squirmed in my arms, already so strong. Then she fixed me with her beady black eyes and I was lost. In a few minutes she filled me with more hope and more despair than I'd felt in every day of my pointless life so far.

CROW appears to Creon.

CREON Crow, I don't have time for this.

CROW Then let's get quickly to the crux of the matter. You're ashamed. I can smell it in your veins. I can smell disgrace like a rancid infection oozing towards the ventricles of your heart.

CREON I have nothing to be ashamed of.

CROW The girl Antigone is right. You could have fought harder for Polynice. You could fight harder for all of them.

CREON What's the point, when no-one's listening? No-one's changing. I spell reform like unicorn.
U. N. I. C. O. R. N.

CROW laughs wildly.

CREON It's not that funny.

CROW I know. I know.

CREON Is that all?

CROW Is it enough?

CREON Am I supposed to know?

CROW leaves

~

CHORUS	Did you see the photo of the girl who died?
	Poor orphaned mite
	Poor innocent child

~

CREON	Haemon! Bring me the girl who shares her cell with Antigone.
HAEMON	Ismene.
CREON	We have a traitor here. News of the death of Polynice has leaked outside The Facility walls.

~

CHORUS	Grasp slipping
	Narrative shifting
	Tragic Foundling Fleeing Brutalisation

~

CREON	Sympathy will spread amongst the citizens like a contagion.

~

CHORUS	Polynice
	Fell into bad hands
	A heart-breaking story
	A helpless young victim
	She should have been nurtured

and welcomed

not side-lined

and shunned

Poor innocent victim

Who's to blame?

Call for an inspection!

~

CREON The System shrinks from scrutinisation: I'll be their scapegoat.

~

CHORUS Fail The Facility

Find the bad apple

Point the finger

Scorn

Blame the governor

Contempt

Shame the governor

Derision

War Child Dies In Failing Prison

~

CREON There will be moments that appear like the mood has shifted. What the citizens have felt apathy for all their lives, may suddenly transform into empathy when the newshounds print the right mawkish image. If such an image of Polynice is leaked, the citizens will weep buckets of sentimental tears; they will clamour for answers.

~

CHORUS Gullible Guv's Secret Shame

Crooked Creon's Rotten Regime

Corrupt Guv Fails Fallen Miscreants

~

CREON The System will make sure I am hung out to dry to satisfy the citizens' outrage.

HAEMON Not if we add our voices to the outrage! An outpouring of empathy from the citizens would strengthen my call for reform; if they are capable of compassion, they're capable of forcing change.

CREON The System won't be forced.

HAEMON At some point, the balance must tip.

CREON Don't overestimate the resolve of the citizens. Their passions pass quickly. Attention spans are short and citizens are easy to appease. The System will guide them back into their little boxes with promises of something sweet or salty. And soon, soon, apathy returns. Even the most shocking image fades and nothing truly changes.

HAEMON But if it suits The System to keep our minds shut and our voices silent, then the fault is with The System and not with us. Antigone is right. It must be possible to wake the citizens up and work with them.

CREON So now you're taking lessons from a charmless little girl?

HAEMON The point she makes is valid. We choose to be mute. We choose to be blind.

CREON Haemon, let's imagine I oppose The System. They will deal with me efficiently. They will either silence me or turn the tide against me. Either way, I will be gone and no use to anyone: not to you, not to the guards, not to the miscreants. A rebel leader who is not there to lead is no leader at all.

HAEMON A leader with no courage or vision is no leader at all.

CREON If we allow Antigone and her band of miscreants to control the narrative, Polynice will flicker for a moment as a tragic hero. There will be a howl of sound and fury and then nothing will change.

HAEMON Nothing will change if we are too afraid to try.

CROW enters.

CROW Nothing will change if you are too afraid to try.

CREON I will make a statement. I will tell the truth about Polynice. Haemon, bring Ismene to me.

HAEMON Ismene, Governor Creon has asked to speak to you.

ISMENE Where's Antigone?

HAEMON In isolation.

ISMENE The more Governor Creon punishes Antigone, the more guilty he seems.

HAEMON Be careful Ismene. Creon is like a trapped tiger. (*QUIETLY*) Your future is in his hands.

ISMENE What future is that?

CREON Enter.

HAEMON enters with ISMENE.

CREON Commiserations on the death of your friend.

ISMENE Thank you, sir.

CREON I hear you share your cell with Antigone?

ISMENE Yes sir.

CREON Ismene, I need you to do something for me. There's a crowd gathering outside the gate. The news hounds are demanding a statement from me and I'm fearful that the tragic passing of Polynice will turn into some ridiculous spectacle. It's important that the message that reaches the citizens is measured and respectful as would be expected in these grave and sorry circumstances.

ISMENE Antigone says Polynice would still be alive if her claim for sanctuary had been accepted.

CREON Antigone and the truth are dangerous strangers. I've prepared a statement that will put an end to the unpleasant gossip and restore dignity to our grief. I want you to read it to the press.

ISMENE Antigone would be better at this.

CREON I don't think so.

CREON hands ISMENE a piece of paper.

ISMENE (*READING*) On behalf of everyone at The Facility, I want to express our deepest sadness at the tragic passing of Polynice. May she sleep peacefully and find, in sleep, redemption.

CREON Continue.

ISMENE My own time here has taught me the value of law and order and I look forward to completing my transformation from misguided miscreant to valuable citizen within the walls of The Facility.

CREON Continue.

ISMENE What if I won't read it? What if I won't read your statement?

CREON Listen Ismene. You have lived long enough and in tough enough times to know how The Realm works; it is rarely kind to young single mothers like you. Your baby daughter was born to you in The Facility and swiftly taken away: another blow to your chance of happiness. Taking on such a duty as this will look good for you at your next review. The panel will respond well to any recommendations from me and I predict a swift and simple path to release.

ISMENE Why should I believe you?

CREON What choice do you have? There's nothing you can do to help Polynice now and to refuse to do this won't help Antigone. Or your baby. Haemon, please escort Ismene back to her cell to prepare for the press conference. She should dress to give the impression of demure repentance.

HAEMON leads Ismene away. GUARD 2 passes with ANTIGONE in handcuffs.

ISMENE Antigone!

ANTIGONE They're taking me to court Ismene! Creon is charging me for speaking my mind!

ISMENE No!

ANTIGONE I'll be re-sentenced and transferred.

ISMENE I'll write to you. I'll find you.

ANTIGONE I'll be sent to The Reformatory.

ISMENE No! They can't do that. I won't let you rot between the walls of a cell.

ANTIGONE You made your choice Ismene. A woman's role is to stay in the box she's put in. You've acted exactly as they expect you to.

ISMENE Don't leave like this.

ANTIGONE Go mother your baby. Go sing her lullabies. Sing them out so loud that she won't hear her hopeless, helpless future lumbering towards her.

ANTIGONE is dragged off by GUARD 2.

HAEMON is left listening to ISMENE singing a lullaby. One by one the CHORUS join in.

ISMENE Lullaby and goodnight
Go to sleep now and dream,
Close your eyes,
Close your mind,
Leave your troubles far behind.
If the sun lights the skies,
you will wake feeling fine.
If the sun lights the skies,
you will wake feeling fine.
If the sun –

ISMENE stops singing abruptly.

GUARD 2 Here are the clothes that Creon wants you to wear.

HAEMON I can't breathe.

~

CHORUS Transform

~

HAEMON I can't breathe in here.

Throughout CREON'S meeting with CROW, the MISCREANTS help ISMENE dress. At first, traditionally feminine clothes are layered on top of ISMENE'S standard prison clothes but as the scene continues, the clothes start to restrict her movements and obscure her from view.

CROW pulls up a chair for a heart to heart with CREON.

CROW What's new, my friend?

CREON My son has abandoned me.

CROW Coward.

CREON There are crowds of citizens outside. If they start howling, I'll be thrown to them.

CROW Many a martyr has been thrown to the dogs.

CREON Polynice is dead. Antigone is silenced.

CROW	A strong leader must be strong.
CREON	I should have sent the letters of support.

~

CHORUS	Should have. Could have. Would have.

~

CREON	I should have written the report.
CROW	You were busy.
CREON	It should have been a priority.
CROW	You were far too busy.
CREON	I could have made it a priority.
CROW	But your list was long. Your daughter needed to speak to you about her marriage troubles. Seven of your B Wing staff were off sick. The frozen chips weren't delivered to the kitchen. There was a fight on C Wing.
CREON	Whose side are you on?
CROW	There weren't enough officers to staff the night shift. You didn't cause the leak in D Wing bathroom.

Or fail to turn up to fix it.

~

CHORUS There's always an excuse to not do what should have been done.

~

CROW You didn't plan to have a headache that slammed around your skull like miscreants in a stolen car.

You didn't mean to forget to submit her claim for sanctuary.

CREON I didn't even think about it. Until her deportment forms came through, I didn't once think of it. Antigone is right.

CROW Then pardon her.

Fifth Stasimon

POLYNICE leads the CHORUS in a dance.

POLYNICE

more than skin to skin and lip to lip
love lasts longer than borders and is stronger than kings

my feet stamped fresh grief across burnt earth
my heart sailed peacock seas turning stormy inside me

I took a handful of home earth
to spell my name to strangers if I washed up unclaimed

muscles wrestle for supremacy
where weakened egos scream, with blank eyes, for blind worship

I dreamt of another city's stage
on which to quietly rest my wrecked and shattered wings

~

CREON

Crow. Shut the doors. Shut all the doors.

CROW Listen Creon. We can all change. Look at me: in the slick black of my feathers are petrol purples and peacock greens.

Exodus

CREON leads ISMENE forward, still restricted by the clothing she is dressed in. HAEMON and GUARD 1 step between CREON and ISMENE.

HAEMON Ismene. Breathe. Breathe deeply.

The MISCREANTS form a circle around ISMENE. The CHORUS are quiet for once. ISMENE makes a paper bird from Creon's statement and launches it into the crowd. She then speaks her own words out loud.

ISMENE I sacrifice my daughter for you Antigone: a sacrifice you asked of me. I sacrifice my freedom for you Polynice: a price you never wanted any of us to pay. I sing a lullaby to my child but not to soothe her to sleep. Daughter, it is a song to wake you up. Wake up to poverty, prejudice and injustice. Point a finger at those in power when they behave badly. Ask questions. Take responsibility. Find kindred spirits to connect across differences. Open your mind to voices of dissent and your heart to change. Don't get comfy. Don't let the drone of everyday defeat you. Don't accept hope unless it helps drive an engine burning inside you. Get hungry. Get angry. Stamp your feet and sing out loud, louder, loudest.

~

POLYNICE my feet stamp fresh grief across burnt earth

my heart sails peacock seas turning stormy inside me

~

CROW What will you say Creon?

CREON is silent

ANTIGONE We, who were born not to think

and not to speak

must open our mouths.

Now, Ismene.

Listen.

ISMENE Polynice is dead but not forgotten.

~

POLYNICE more than skin to skin and lip to lip

love lasts longer than borders and is stronger than kings

THE END

REFLECTIONS ON THE PLAY

Writing any adaptation is like drawing a map from the original to your own version. At each intersection, you make a choice about which way you want to go; the final destination depends on your focus, your interests, your emotional response, your personal experience and your research.

I started my map with the girl herself: Antigone. I read articles, listened to podcasts and ordered every adaptation of her story that I could get my hands on. I learnt what she meant to audiences across the centuries and why her story still moves people today. Antigone stood out to me as a rebel girl, willing to risk everything for what she believed in.

As I read Sophocles' play, I scribbled ideas in notebooks and on index cards. I recorded voice notes to myself whilst walking the dog. Sometimes, I talked to the dog, asking him what he thought about making Creon's conscience into a blind crow. Before writing any scenes, I slept on ideas, daydreamed characters into existence and let the conflict and themes that were brewing in my head clash against the ordinary everyday of living.

At first, Antigone and Creon filled my thoughts. Both are larger than life: powerful and stubborn in their own way. Antigone is brave and tenacious but her treatment of Ismene bothered me. Creon is angry and oppressive and yet, I began to feel a reluctant sympathy for him. Gradually, Ismene and Haemon emerged as quieter characters with something important to say.

I decided to set my version of *Antigone* in The Facility because I've worked in prisons and know them as intense microsocieties where a conflict between two strong characters can be explosive. Antigone as inmate and Creon as prison governor felt like a rich dynamic to explore, full of potential for drama and social comment.

The key themes are disturbingly relevant today: inequality, patriarchy, poverty and shame. In *The Facility*, Antigone is determined to learn the truth about the death of Polynice. By taking on Creon, she is fighting for all marginalised voices – including her own. Her struggle draws out the themes of resilience, resistance, creativity and loyalty.

I am a poet as well as a script writer so the structure and style of Sophocles' *Antigone* appealed to me. I began plotting my story around seven scenes and six choral songs: my scenes advance the narrative while the choral songs play with language and form – often with a direct nod to the original as in 'Ode to Man.'

In later drafts, I allowed the Chorus, Crow and the ghost of Polynice to drift from the choral songs into the scenes, blurring the lines between poetry and prose: between narrative and comment. I created rules for myself that I broke – sometimes to create an unexpected juxtaposition or interruption: sometimes to deliberately encourage the audience to reflect mid-action.

At times, particularly with the Chorus, I have used punctuation as it's used in poetry: to emphasise the rhythm, to suggest a pause or to foreground a particular point. Feel free to play with these choices in your performance as you experiment with meaning and delivery.

I have kept stage directions to a minimum because this is your play to interpret and make relevant to your lives. Creon may be dressed as a clown. The chorus could be played by puppets. Gender roles might be reversed. Sing. Shout. Dance. Keep the stage bare or fill it with balloons to be popped throughout the performance. Have fun. Be brave. Make your voices heard.

Sarah Hehir

Being Antigone

A story by Barbara Bleiman

It hadn't been a good year. In fact, it had been a terrible one. It was as if the gods were looking at us with angry faces, bearing weapons of war, raining down thunderbolts and lightning from their comfy, cushioned seats up in the heavens. First my nan died. She had a freak accident, a little fall in her kitchen that seemed like nothing. A week later, she was rushed to hospital and never came out. It had been a blood clot in her leg that travelled up to her heart and killed her. My older brothers Pauly and Ethan and my little sister Izzy and I all went to the funeral and put flowers on the coffin. It was tough to see our nan buried but tougher still for mum, who'd relied so much on her. Mum went a bit absent, as if she'd forgotten all of us. She was there but not there, if you see what I mean – there in her body, but not in her mind. Usually, she'd notice the slightest thing. Sometimes it was annoying, sometimes not. 'Not got any homework, Alicia?', 'Looking a bit glum – something up?', 'How's things with that nasty girl in your class, the queen bee?'. But now, she barely seemed aware of anything. The food was on the table, the washing done, the groceries in the cupboard but mum wasn't really with us. She didn't see what else was happening.

So Nan dying was the first bad thing, and then Pauly and Ethan moved out. It'd been coming for quite a while. Mum had stopped arguing with them because of being so sad about Nan, but Dad just took over, now she was out of action. He sort of adopted her role, as if he felt he had to keep up the side, nagging them about their mess, the time they spent on their computers, those layabout friends of theirs who kept coming around, why they weren't working harder to bring in a bit more money, whether the courier company they both worked for would put up with them for much longer given how unreliable they were, and so on and so on. It drove Ethan and Pauly mad – and me too. In his day, he said, young men had more respect. In his day, he said, they put in the hours. In his day, children were less rude to their parents. It was true, Dad had always worked really hard.

He's a plumber, and he gets called out on weekends and even in the middle of the night sometimes. And he'd been really nice to Nan, no matter what, even though she wasn't his own mum, just his mother-in-law. And great about Mum too, trying to support her. Dad was steady. He was strong. Someone to look up to. I could vouch for all that. But he could be very annoying too. Pauly and Ethan rolled their eyes, when he got going on one of his 'In my day…' lectures, or just walked out the room.

After Pauly and Ethan left they didn't come around much – Ethan hardly ever, Pauly a bit more. It was lovely to see him, when he did suddenly turn up, unannounced, give me a big hug and go straight to the fridge to raid it for a piece of cold chicken or whatever else he could find. But it wasn't so often and then it always ended in a row with Dad, so the visits tailed off. A few months later, we heard that Ethan had lost his job. 'What's he living on?' Dad asked. 'How's he paying his rent?' No-one answered. Izzy and I just looked at each other. We kind of knew but didn't want to actually say it out loud. I think Mum and Dad probably knew too, but no-one wanted to admit it, definitely not to each other, maybe not even to ourselves.

And then Carla, one of Mum's friends, came around and said she'd heard something about Ethan having been in trouble with the police. He'd been charged with something or other, she wasn't sure what. That was it, for Mum. The final straw. She disappeared up into her bedroom, crawled under the duvet and stayed there. When I say stayed there, I mean stayed there. Just trips to the loo. Nothing else. Dad took up trays of food and a few hours later brought them back down again. I couldn't help but see how little she'd eaten. It was as if a little bird had been pecking at the food, or a not very hungry mouse nibbling away at the edges.

I went in and sat on the edge of her bed sometimes and held her hand. She squeezed mine and tried to smile, then closed her eyes, or turned away from me.

'He'll be OK,' I said, one time, trying to reassure her, though I was saying things that I couldn't really reassure myself with. 'I'm sure it'll turn out all right in the end.' She didn't say anything, just sighed, and I tiptoed out, gently closing the door behind me.

'You should go and see Ethan,' I said to Dad. 'To give him some help. He's in trouble.'

'Ssshh,' whispered Izzy, 'you'll just cause a row.' Izzy hated a scene – she'd do anything to avoid one.

'He's your son,' I said, ignoring her. I wasn't one to give up so easily. 'He needs you, Dad.' There was silence. 'He's your son, isn't he?' I repeated.

Dad shrugged. 'Some son!' he said. 'Look what he's done to your mother. Perhaps he needs this as a wake-up call. It'll shake him up a bit. We've all been too soft on him. He'll get a good stern warning and then maybe he'll mend his ways and settle down. Anyway, he can come and see me if he wants to. Nobody's stopping him. When was he last over here to see your mother and me? What interest does he show in you and Izzy? None whatsoever.' He picked up his newspaper as if to say the conversation was over as far as he was concerned.

'I'll go and see him myself,' I said.

'No you won't, missy!' he replied in a quiet but determined voice. 'I forbid it. I don't want you having anything to do with him, not till he sorts himself out. If he dragged you into any of his nonsense, it'd be the death of your mother.'

That's why I didn't do it. I didn't go and see my brother. Because I was worried about my mother, I listened to my dad. I bowed down to his judgement. I caved in, without a fight, without so much as a whimper of protest. So, when I heard that Ethan hadn't just been given a warning but had been handed down a sentence, a short stretch of a few months in a Young Offenders' Institution, I felt terrible.

'I should have gone to see him,' I said to Izzy. 'I might have been able to do something.'

'That's silly, Ali. What on earth could you have done?' Izzy said. 'Dad's right. Ethan's been given so many chances. You're only fifteen, anyhow. You couldn't have done anything to help.'

That was true, of course, but I still felt bad. Ethan was my wonderful, big brother. I'd always worshipped him. I had great memories of him from when we were younger. He bought me ice creams and bags of sweets. He took me skateboarding and taught me how to ride backwards and do fakie kickturns and roll down a ramp and never told me to buzz off when his friends came along. He seemed almost proud of me and what I could do. He watched out for me, too. The other kids knew that Ethan was covering my back – the bullies left me alone. And he made me laugh, boy how he made me laugh. I once almost threw up because of it. I loved Izzy and Pauly, of course I did, but with Ethan and me, it was something special. We just clicked.

I said Ethan 'was' my brother. He isn't any more. When Ethan was sent to the Young Offenders' Institution, he couldn't cope with it. He wasn't a tough boy, though he sometimes pretended to other people that he was. He'd only been there a month or so when he took his life.

First Nan, now Ethan. Gods, what on earth have we done wrong? How did we get so badly on the wrong side of you that you decided to punish us like this?

Izzy, being Izzy, cried her eyes out, for nights and days and weeks when we heard about Ethan. She sobbed and sobbed – she let it all out, all her grief. 'I'm so sad,' she whimpered and Dad comforted her. Pauly came back home. He cried too. I hadn't seen that happen for a good many years. I hadn't seen him so destroyed. I didn't cry, though. Not me. I wanted to, but the tears just wouldn't come. I was too angry to cry. Too ashamed. One of us should have done something to stop all this. If not Mum, if not Dad, or even Pauly, then me. I had a pool of sadness and anger and regret that was too deep to swim in safely. If I even put a toe in that dark water I would drown.

So I bottled it up. I didn't tell the teachers, my Form Tutor, Mr Watson, or Miss Margolyes, my Head of Year. Most of my friends knew of course, but after the first day or two, when everyone seemed to be talking about it in the playground or on the way home, I made it clear it wasn't up for discussion. It was my business, not theirs. They were relieved, I think. No-one knew what to say. They were embarrassed. Better to pretend nothing had happened, for them and for me.

I didn't tell them about Mum either. Ethan really was the last straw for her. Mum and Dad both knew she needed help, more than just Dad or the rest of us could give, so she went away. 'Just for a little while,' Dad said. 'We can visit her whenever we like, once she's stabilised a bit. They've put her on some pills.'

'What's wrong with her?' I asked.

Dad was silent, struggling for the right words.

'Nan's death and now Ethan, it's all been too much for her,' he said.

To be honest, Mum hadn't been quite right for a while, even before Nan's death, but I could see that everything that had happened had tipped her right over the edge. But now she'd gone, I was going to have to cope with all this stuff without her. Even knowing she was up in her bedroom was better than her not being there at all. It felt so unfair. My family was a mess. Everything was falling apart. I was angry with Ethan for dying, I was angry with myself for not helping him and now I was really angry with Mum too.

One day, shortly after Mum had gone to the hospital, Mr Watson asked me to stay behind after tutor time.

'What's going on, Alicia?' he asked. He folded his arms and put on his stern face. Stern for Mr Watson wasn't so stern really. It always looked as if he had to try really hard to get it right – it didn't come naturally. I'd had four years to get to know that look well. Usually it made me laugh but this time it didn't seem so funny. 'What's going on?' he repeated.

'Nothing,' I replied.

'You've gone right off the boil these past few weeks,' he said. 'All your teachers have noticed.'

I shrugged.

'You're usually such a great student. Totally reliable. Right up there with the best in the class. But your work's been rubbish the last few weeks. Nothing like what you're capable of.'

Rubbish. I felt the blood rush to my face. Rubbish. What would his work be like if things were as shit for him as they were for me? I said nothing, though, just looked down.

His voice softened a bit. 'Is there something worrying you?'

I shrugged.

'You can tell me you know.'

I shook my head.

'Well, you know I'm here. You can find me if you need to. Just make sure that your work picks up!'

I looked away. I didn't know what to say.

My work didn't pick up. How could it? There was going to be an inquest into Ethan's death in custody and the funeral was delayed. Another thing to worry about. When would the funeral actually happen, and would I be allowed to go? Would Mum get there, and what would it do to her, if she did? So many questions buzzing inside my head like angry bees, driving me mad with their noise and attacking me with their vicious stings. In Maths,

I could barely get from the start of a problem to the end, without losing the thread. In History, I'd usually be first in with a question or a comment, whether on the Slave Trade or the Cold War, but now I just couldn't be bothered. In English, not even my favourite author, Malorie Blackman, could drag my thoughts back into the classroom and onto the pages we were reading. The words just swam around in a sea of meaningless print.

Izzy seemed to be managing better than me. I wondered why. Maybe it was because she was more open. She and Dad seemed to help each other. I wasn't part of that. I didn't like talking about how I felt at the best of times, let alone now. Mum had often accused me of being like an oyster shell, so tightly clamped that it's almost impossible to prise the two parts open. 'And inside there's a lovely little pearl,' Mum used to say, 'hiding away.' It made me smile. I was a pearl, then, in Mum's eyes. Not a slippery, slimy, watery old oyster, but a shiny pearl. Now, thinking of Mum made me gulp back the tears. I needed her right now, to force me out of my shell. I couldn't do it on my own.

'You haven't told the teachers, have you, Izzy?' I asked.

'No,' she said quietly, looking a bit sheepish. There was a pause. 'Only Miss Burton.'

'For goodness sake!' I said. 'Why her? What did you tell her?'

'Just about Ethan…' She was biting her lip like she sometimes does when she's nervous. '…And about Mum.'

I couldn't believe it. Miss Burton was my favourite teacher. She taught me Drama, my best subject. I wanted her to like me and I definitely didn't want her thinking I came from a family who were in all kinds of trouble. Which we were, of course. I really wanted her respect. And now Izzy had gone and told her everything, and all the other teachers would get to know too.

'For fuck's sake, Izzy!'

She tried to reach out and touch my hand but I whipped it back quickly, turned on my heel, stormed off upstairs to our bedroom and slammed the door so hard that the poster tacked on the back flapped wildly for a moment, and then slid gracefully to the floor.

Almost immediately, my anger started to subside and I began to feel guilty. It wasn't Izzy's fault. I wanted to tell her that she had every right to talk to whoever she wanted, if it would help, that it was fine. I wanted to say all of that, but I couldn't. And I knew I wouldn't. I just lay there on my bed wondering what we'd all done to deserve this. And worst of all was knowing that I was handling it so badly. I was making things worse.

That evening, instead of apologising, I made Izzy's favourite meal – meatballs and pasta. I hoped that, even though I couldn't bring myself to say anything, she'd realise why and what it meant.

It was the following Tuesday that Miss Burton asked me to stay behind after the Drama lesson. I knew what was going to happen. She was going to ask me to tell her all about Ethan and Mum, and then I'd have to answer her questions without crying, and I really, really didn't think I could.

'I can't stay Miss,' I said quickly, 'I'm meeting someone.'

'Just for a minute,' she insisted.

I had no choice.

She sat perched on the edge of her desk. She took her glasses off, as she often does when she means business, and blinked a few times, like she does when she's a bit nervous.

'I've got a favour to ask of you,' she said, straightaway.

'A favour?' I wasn't expecting that. What could the wonderful Miss B want from me? It was usually her doing favours for other people, I thought – she was that nice, and that kind.

'I'm in a bit of a pickle.'

'A pickle?'

Here I was repeating every word she said. She must think I'd completely lost the plot.

'Well you know how I'm putting on a play at the end of next term, and how you ruled yourself out when we did the auditions – you made it clear that you didn't want to put yourself forward… Well, I was really disappointed, you knew that. I told you so. I thought you'd be a great member of the cast. But you decided it'd be too much for you, with all your school work, and, other things and you didn't audition…' She paused. I wondered what she was going to say. 'I respected your decision, Alicia. It wasn't right for you at the time.'

I nodded. 'Thanks Miss.'

'Well now, as I say, I'm in a pickle. The girl taking the lead role has broken her ankle playing football. She can't do it in a plaster cast. So I have no main character. Well, I immediately thought of you.'

'No, Miss,' I said, 'The timing's even worse now. I really couldn't do it.'

Miss Burton sighed. 'The timing may well be worse, it may be awful…,' she said. I waited for her to say more. She looked at me hard. 'But sometimes, however bad the timing, you have to do something because it's worth doing. You do it because it's the right thing. It needs to be done. You show determination, strength of character, guts.'

'I can't,' I said firmly. 'I just can't.' And rather than giving her the chance to try to persuade me, I picked up my bag and left. Just like that.

I wondered about skipping the next Drama lesson rather than face her again. I'd just stormed off the last time I saw her.

What would she be thinking of me? But when the lesson came around I decided to go. I liked her and I really liked the lessons. Bunking off would be a step too far. So I turned up, leaving my entry as late as possible, to avoid having her say anything to me.

The space was arranged differently from usual. There were tables and chairs set out, rather than the usual open performance space in the middle of the room.

'Today we're going to do something a bit different,' she said. 'We're putting that last theme of friendship to one side. We'll do some improv a bit later, as usual, but first I want to read you a speech from a play. I'm going to tell you a little bit about it and then I'm just going to read it to you. While I'm reading it, I want you to listen and think about it. Think about what leaps out at you, what interests you, what it reminds you of, what it makes you feel.' She paused.

'Here's a little bit of context for you before I read the speech,' she said. 'It's set in Greece, in ancient times. Creon is a very powerful ruler. His word goes. He makes an order forbidding a young woman from burying her brother, who has been killed in a fight with her other brother. The girl ignores that order and undertakes the burial with her own bare hands. Creon is outraged at her disobedience. He asks if she heard his order, and confirms that she did. 'And yet,' Creon says angrily, 'you disobeyed my law.' The young woman replies with this speech.

Yes, I did. Because it's your law,
Not the law of god. Natural justice,
Which is of all times and places, numinous,
Not material, a quality of Zeus,
Not of kinds, recognises no such law.
You are merely a man, mortal,
Like me, and laws that you enact
Cannot overturn ancient moralities

Of common human decency.
They speak the language of eternity,
Are not written down, and never change.
They are for today, yesterday, and all time.
No one understands where they came from,
But everyone recognises their force:
And no man's arrogance or power
Can make me disobey them. I would rather
Suffer the disapproval and punishment
Of men, than dishonour such ancient truths.'

Miss Burton stopped. I would have liked her to read it again. I wanted to hear more. I didn't understand it all but I thought I got enough of the gist to know that it was a girl talking about burying her dead brother, about standing up for decency, a young girl obeying something more important than the commands of a ruler or the expectations of those around her. I sat totally still, as if I'd been turned to stone. All around me, students were starting to jot down their thoughts but my notebook stayed shut, my pen lay unused in my hand. I couldn't write a single word of what I was thinking, not one. Inside my exterior of stone, a volcano was stirring and bubbling. I knew that if the lid of the stone mountain blew, hot lava would erupt all over the page.

Miss Burton asked if anyone wanted to tell the class their thoughts. Millie asked what 'eternity' meant, and Zeus too. Miss B explained that eternity was forever and Zeus was the all-powerful chief of the gods. Aysha said she thought the girl was brave. Jamal said it reminded him of a play we'd read in English about standing up for your beliefs. Jake jumped in and said it made him think of Greta Thunberg. Miss Burton asked why and Jake said she was brave and said publicly what had to be said on climate change and stood up against world leaders. Lola, under her breath as usual, almost whispered that it made her feel a bit sad and quite impressed with the girl, all at the same time.

Miss Burton nodded. 'Yes, she said. 'It's sad but also inspiring isn't it? She isn't afraid. That's what tragedies are often like, not only Greek tragedies – Shakespeare too. You feel sad about the awful things that happen to the characters but you also feel something else. Something big and powerful is going on, that, as Lola says, makes you feel sorry for the hero or heroine, but also impressed by them.'

She would usually ask me for my thoughts if I was quiet in class discussion but this time she didn't. She didn't even look at me. I wondered why, but to be honest I was really relieved. I couldn't have trusted myself to say anything.

'This speech comes from a play by an ancient Greek playwright called Sophocles,' she said. 'It's called *Antigone*. That's the name of the young girl. I thought you might be interested in it because it's the source of the play we're putting on next term. We'll be doing a modern version, a spin-off from it, not the Greek one. The original play is quite adult and maybe a bit too tragic for the whole school to watch and for the actors to handle. The Antigone in our play doesn't disobey Creon and bury her brother but she does have some difficult challenges and she does some pretty amazing things. She's a tough cookie, our Antigone!'

Antigone. Miss B said it like this – Antigonee. I liked the sound of the name. I hadn't a clue what it meant, if anything, but it was unusual and interesting. Anti. That meant against. She was against what was happening, against the rules and against the ruler. She disobeyed him because she didn't believe in what he stood for. Her name reminded me of the word 'agony' too. Agony. That's what I was going through. Like me, her brother had died and he'd not been buried. She'd not been able to mourn him properly. Agony. She wanted to do what was right for her brother. She wanted to bury him. And then there was the 'gone' bit in her name. He'd gone. Her brother, that is. He'd died. But she'd gone too, to a different place, where she was out on her own, cut off from other people. She'd broken the rules so she was a rebel, an outsider. She'd gone beyond the limits. Gone too far. Whether it actually meant any of that didn't really matter. That's what it meant to me. Antigone.

I wanted to hear more of the play, but Miss Burton was already clearing away the chairs and tables and making a space for the improv. That was usually my favourite bit of the lessons. But this time, I sat in one of the darkened corners of the room and let other people jump into the brightly lit spotlight. The idea for this improv was all about 'the absurd' – normal, everyday situations which are odd in some way. A bus stop with zoo animals waiting in line, a teenager behaving and talking like a parent, a shop that only sold one thing, serving a string of very confused customers. Maybe Miss B thought she needed to lighten the mood a bit, after the seriousness of that Antigone speech.

At home that evening I googled Antigone. I read the Wikipedia summary of the play and sat stunned. A dead brother mourned. A dead brother unburied. A young girl who breaks Creon's laws to bury him and ends up killing herself. The man who loves her, son of Creon, killing himself too, out of grief, and his mother, Creon's wife, doing the same. And then Creon realising what a terrible set of events he'd set in motion by decreeing that Antigone's brother should be denied burial, acting against the will of the gods and the ancient beliefs and customs of the people. Bleak, dark stuff. Tragic events. An awful, awful ending, with so much grief and so many people dead. I couldn't help thinking about them and about me and my family. Horrible stuff had happened to us – to me – and was still happening. What was our 'ending' going to be? And anyway, was there such a thing as an ending in real life, or would this trauma just carry on forever, an 'eternity' of sadness and awful things happening to us?

Later that week, I managed to go and see my Mum for the first time. The hospital wasn't so bad – not as grim as I'd expected – and seeing her was good too. She was sitting up in a chair, in a bright room, no curtains closed, her bed neat and tidy, reading a magazine. The minute she saw Izzy and me, her eyes lit up. We went to give her a hug and she opened her arms. For a few moments we remained there, wrapped in her warmth. We didn't stay at the hospital very long – Dad said to keep the first visit short. But it was something. Mum cried while we were there. She seemed upset, more so than when she was hidden in her duvet, at home, not doing or saying anything at all. On the way home, Dad said that was definitely progress. Perhaps he was right. I wasn't sure.

The next day, at lunchtime, I went to find Miss Burton in her room. She was eating a sandwich from a plastic box. She welcomed me in.

'What can I do for you, Alicia?'

'Can you tell me about the new version of Antigone, the one you're doing as the school play?'

Miss Burton looked at me. She hesitated, as if she were going to ask me something. And then she didn't. 'Just wait here,' she said. She got up and went to her store cupboard and unlocked it. I sat waiting for ages, wondering what she was up to. I could hear her humming to herself. Finally, she came back holding an A4 sheaf of paper, bound in a plastic folder. 'Here it is,' she said. 'The script. My spare copy. Take it away and read it. But I'll need it back by Thursday. I'm going to be auditioning a few people for Antigone then, and they'll need the speech I'm going to try them out on.'

'Is it like the one you read out in class?'

'No. It's different. But it's equally passionate. See if you can spot the speech I've chosen!'

At school the next day, at lunchtime I went to the Drama Studio.

'Why do you keep going there?' my friends asked. They wondered what was going on. What was I up to? I told them I'd borrowed something from my teacher and needed to return it.

Miss Burton was there, eating what looked like exactly the same sandwiches as before, from the same plastic box.

'Alicia,' she said. 'Good to see you! Have you got that script for me?'

I took it out of my bag.

'That's great. Thank you. I hope you enjoyed it. See you next Tuesday at Drama!'

I was taken aback. What had I expected? Well, at the very least I'd hoped she might ask what I thought of the play. I thought she would question me about the ending. Then I could have asked for her view, to help me to make more sense of it. I didn't expect her to just take the script and send me away. I'd hoped for a chat about it, at the very least, maybe something more.

I went out into the corridor and down towards the staircase. I was about to go down and make my way towards the canteen where my friends were all eating their lunch. But something made me stop. I stood there for a good few minutes, then turned back towards the Drama Studio, and before I could change my mind, I knocked on the door.

Miss Burton didn't seem surprised to see me back again so quickly.

'Is it a sad ending, Miss?' I said. 'I didn't think so, but I wanted to know what you thought.'

'It's complicated,' she replied. 'It depends a bit on how it's played, how the actors and the director choose to present it. It's like what Lola said, it's a bit sad but it's also very impressive. How sad, how impressive? That's up to the cast.'

'What will yours be like?' I asked.

'It depends on my Antigone,' she said, 'and what she brings to the role.'

'I think you should audition her with the speech to the crowd,' I said. 'I think that's her best moment.'

'That's the one I've chosen, Alicia. That's my favourite too.'

I was smiling now.

'That speech goes really well with the old one too, the Greek one you read us in class.'

'It does,' Miss Burton said. 'It gives such a good sense of what Antigone is made of. Her courage, her convictions, her unusual strength of character. Suffering and sorrow bring out what's most noble in her.'

I nodded. 'She's amazing,' I said.

I walked towards the door again. She was going to just let me go.

'Can I audition for her, miss?' I said finally.

'Of course,' she said, smiling. '1pm tomorrow, here in the studio.'

***

So, that's how I came to be Antigone. The new one, not the old one. I never needed to be reminded to learn my lines – they jumped off the pages into my head and they stayed there. Some, I knew, I would never, ever forget. They'd be with me for life.

Dad wondered whether it was a good idea, what with all we'd been going through. Wouldn't it put too much strain on me? I agreed to let him go and talk to Mr Watson and Miss Burton, and the school counsellor, to see what they thought. I wanted to go too, but they suggested a first meeting with him on his own. And then maybe I'd want to see the school counsellor myself, for a short period? Usually, I'd have said I didn't need help from a counsellor, thank you very much. But if I could be Antigone, then maybe it'd be worth it. I said I'd think about it.

Dad came back smiling after the meeting. 'That Miss Burton has so much faith in you,' he said. 'She sees only the good in you.' He paused. 'Lucky she doesn't see your pigsty of a room, hear you swearing at Izzy, have to put up with your bad TV choices and your terrible table manners!' I laughed, for the first time in ages. 'They've suggested you try the role for a couple of weeks and see how you manage. If the pressure's too much, they'll let someone else have a go.'

There was pressure, no doubt about it and there were a few tricky things to negotiate. I had to ask for one of the rehearsal days to be changed so I could visit Mum at the hospital. The thing I thought would be most difficult of all – Miss Burton talking to me about Ethan and Mum – turned out to be fine. She occasionally asked me how things were going with Mum but usually just left it to me to say something if I wanted to. I found myself telling her, one day, at the end of the rehearsal, that the inquest on Ethan's death had finally happened, and they'd recorded a verdict of death by suicide. They'd decided there was no negligence by the authorities at the Young Offenders' Institution. He'd been on suicide watch at night but somehow he'd taken his chance during a change of shift. I wasn't sure whether that was the right verdict or not. How could any of us know? But at least now he could be properly buried. And the funeral would be in a few weeks' time.

The week before the funeral, I went to see Miss Burton at lunchtime. Same sandwiches, same plastic box. I told her that I'd made a decision. I could see her forehead furrow with anxiety and her eyes blinked furiously – a tell-tale sign of her nervousness.

'What is it?' she said. 'You've not changed your mind about being Antigone, have you?'

I laughed. 'No,' I said. 'I'm definitely Antigone. What I've decided is that I want to say something at Ethan's funeral. I'd like to perform that speech from the play that I did for the audition. I want to know what you think of that idea?'

I thought I knew Miss Burton, but I had never seen this look on her face before. Her eyes weren't blinking at all, they were just filled with tears. She waited a moment to collect herself, gulped a bit and then said,

'I think that's a really wonderful idea.'

***

Dad, and Pauly and Izzy and I were all at the funeral. Mum came too. Dad said some lovely things about Ethan, and Pauly spoke as well. Mum and Izzy sat together, and I sat with Dad and Pauly, close to the front, because I was going to be one of the speakers. When it came to it, I didn't just recite Antigone's speech. I prepared something else as well. So, first I talked about Ethan and the ice creams and sweets, and the skateboarding and how he'd been such a brilliant brother to me. And then I said how I wanted him to be remembered always for those things, not for the time when things went so wrong for him. And finally, I spoke the speech and I gave it my all. It was Antigone's speech but it was mine too. I was Antigone.

When I came down from the podium, I looked over towards Mum. She was sobbing. Sobbing her heart out. But she beckoned me over and I went to sit next to her and she kissed me. Throughout the rest of the service she held my hand. Later Dad came and gave me a big hug and told me how proud he was of me.

Did the play we performed for the school have a happy ending? I played it as if it did. Miss Burton directed it that way too. There'd been a lot of sadness, but in the end, Antigone proved herself. She showed what an amazingly strong and resolute girl she was. She wasn't bowed down. And you could tell that she was going to go on and do amazing things in her life.

Did my story have a happy ending? Well, yes and no. The play was a great success and everyone said what a good job I did in the lead role. Dad and Izzy and Pauly all came to watch it. In fact, Dad came two nights in a row. He said he couldn't believe what a good little actor I was. 'You've got a real talent for it,' he said. I was thrilled. I agreed with Miss Burton that the following year I'd audition for the National Youth Theatre. It would be tough competition, she said, but I said I didn't mind. I'd give it a go, whatever my chances. I was determined to try.

So that was the happy side. I started to see that whatever had happened in my life so far, things could be good and they could be bad. There were ups and downs, swings and roundabouts, snakes and ladders. The gods weren't always good to you, but sometimes, if you gave them just a small prod, or smiled up at them, buttering them up a bit to get them on your side, they'd put some good luck your way.

Mum didn't come and see me in the play. That was the unhappy side of things. She wasn't well enough for that. It took her a good few years more to come out of her depression and start to feel like her old self again. It made me sad, of course, and it worried me, and I wished so much that she would get better faster. But I didn't let it ruin everything else. I tried to just get on with things and make the most of them. I tried to be glad about the good things – Dad, Izzy, Pauly, my acting. I tried to be strong. And mostly, I managed it. I was Antigone, after all.

REFLECTIONS ON THE STORY

Antigone is a really powerful play; it seems to me to have a huge amount of relevance to our society and to young people today, as it has had to young people in many different times and places since it was written hundreds of years ago. In writing a short story inspired by it, I wanted to tap into some of the themes of the play but also to create a female protagonist of my own who deals with the suffering and conflict in her modern life, with the same passion, intelligence and resilience as the Antigone of the Greek play, but whose qualities allow her to overcome adversity rather than being destroyed by it. In my story, ideas about family loyalty, justice, conflict and doing what's right are all played out in a contemporary setting and I enjoyed being able to bring Sophocles' play and the story of Alicia into juxtaposition with each other, using the performance of the ancient play as a way of drawing parallels between the two.

The Dragon and the Girl
A Time

Two poems by Valerie Bloom

The Dragon and the Girl

1.

The Girl

The dragon has roared, he has crawled from his lair,
And the heat of his breath has scorched the pure air.
He has crowned himself God and has made his decree,
Let others bow and cower, I will not bend a knee.

Death is the punishment he means to inflict,
On those who would dare to defy his edict.
But there are laws which are higher; ones I must obey,
For the price of defiance is too high to pay.

Should I leave my dear brother to rot in the street?
To be food for the dogs and the scavenger's meat?
Our good name in the dirt, our honour in ruin?
What of my duty to my God and my kin?

I'm compelled to ignore a law so unjust,
I'll not give in to coercion, I'll die if I must,
And go to my grave with a conscience that's clear,
There was never a law like this passed anywhere!

2.

The Dragon

She has broken the law, and she has been caught,
She's stubborn, she's headstrong, and she must be taught
That her duty is first to her state and her king,
Rebellion in a woman is a dangerous thing.

Like the egg of the viper, revolt should be crushed,
And the voice of dissent immediately hushed,
So soon she will know the result of defiance,
And the wisdom of feminine, submissive compliance.

She has spurned all entreaties, ignored good advice,
She must have a death-wish, and has tried to entice
Her sister to join her in this attack on the state,
And now she will learn of the terrible fate

That awaits those who'd challenge the authority
Of the appointed ruler, and that ruler is me,
I am the state and as such I'm the law,
And I expect everyone to regard me with awe.

3.

Voices

Heaven has spoken and will have the last word,
He who'd bury the living and leave the dead uninterred,
Has been condemned to endure a living death,
Cursing his stupidity with each painful breath,
No woman will better me, he said, taunting,
But he's been weighed in the balance and found wanting.

A Time

It was a time when young women
Should be seen and not heard,
When the thought of a mere girl
Defying the king was absurd,
For females were obedient, submissive, demure,
All injustice and slights they should meekly endure.

So what was she thinking by flouting convention,
By challenging her uncle, the King and the State?
She had overturned order, forgotten her station,
Was she mad or just seeking attention? But wait!

It was a time when young women
Who were seen as well-bred,
Should perform all the
Burial rites for the dead,
Show familial allegiance, religious devotion
So preserving her family's good reputation.

So what was he thinking by flouting convention,
The dead offered as feast for the vulture and kite?
Left in the street, unmourned and unburied,
Blasting the nostrils, repelling the sight.

It was a time when justice
Did not linger long,
Were they both right?
Or was each of them wrong?
For breaking his law the girl paid with her life,
His was wrecked by the deaths of his son and his wife.

The sentence was passed and he was reproved,
And those looking on wondering, astonished and moved,
Said, 'Today it has happened here. With our own eyes
We have seen an old man, through suffering, become wise'.

REFLECTIONS ON THE POEMS

As I read *Antigone*, it struck me how similar some of the plot is to an account in the book of *Revelations* in the Bible. In *Revelations* Chapter 12:9 a dragon (who is 'the Devil and Satan') persecutes a woman and makes a law forcing the whole world to worship in the way he dictates – symbolically he's a dictator who behaves like a dragon. Creon's words reminded me of that, and of legends such as the story of St George and the Dragon, where maidens were tyrannised by dragons. Creon's law seemed quite draconian, and though the word comes from Draco who made repressive laws in ancient Athens, it also conjures the image of a dragon. Hence the title for the first poem.

I thought I would follow the form of the play with the three main actors, Creon, Antigone and the chorus so that it could be a performance poem.

For the second poem, I wanted to explore the themes a bit more and especially the different roles of men and women as brought out in the play. I was also interested in the exploring the characters' motivations for their actions. Did the motives justify the deeds?

The poem is a commentary, a little like that of the chorus in the play, and I left the final words to them.

I often write different versions of the same poem, trying out forms, styles and language before deciding on a final version. Sometimes I'll only use one version, but other times, as in this case, I end up with more than one.

Valerie Bloom

Rage Against the Machine

A poem by Inua Ellams

Rage Against the Machine

Portrait of Antigone and the city

This is my freckled forehead
These are its deep lines
This is the faint meeting of eyebrows
These are my tired eyes
These are its dark waters
These are its grey bags and weighted worries
This is my narrow neck and its heavy duty
This is my throat
This is its forming song
These are my quiet shoulders and simple arms
This its trembling work

Those are the courts of the city
Those are its laws glinting
Those are its chambers combusting
Those judges grease its work
Those leaders fuel its fire
Those officers churn its pistons
Those journalists belch its voice
Those activists spin its raging wheels
This is its fixed course

This is my brother's chest
This is his flat heart
These are his petal-thin eyelids
This oil will scent his soul
This white cloth is a fallen flag
I will place it over his body
I will pray his name
And I will sleep

REFLECTIONS ON THE POEM

It is said the Greek tragedy of *Antigone* has captured audiences for centuries because it dramatises so many conflicts: man versus woman, gods versus humanity, society versus the individual, youth versus age, the living versus the dead. But I have been drawn to something that runs between all of those – fragility versus strength.

We live in a world of power and energy, smoke and steam, metal and iron. Our mechanical and technological innovations are constantly breaking new ground and increasing human capability; however, the hardware of human brain and body has not changed and what we carry can weigh us down. I wanted to draw attention to that in this poem, to show the physical toll of Antigone's decision on her body and to hold that against the machine of the city; to paint the picture of the inevitable collision, and Antigone's final choice.

Inua Ellams

I Heard One Cry in the Night

A story by Phoebe Roy

Month 1: Bukátios

January is the worst month. It was last January when the fight happened, when that girl said I'd attacked her, and her mother went to the police. It wasn't true, of course it wasn't. What had happened was this: it wasn't something I'd started – I was trying to help someone else, another girl I know who was being bothered. All I'd said was that I would handle it, and I thought I could do it quietly. I'd never planned much more than having a word, but then more and more people showed up, and it escalated. If I don't sound clear it's because I really don't remember – just that I was in the middle of it all, all sounds blurred out into one muffled roar, the bridge of the girl's nose blossoming briefly, beautifully red under my fist. Time slowed down and sped up again, and for one short second I stepped outside of my body and saw my limbs wheeling and dancing down there on the ground.

I wonder if that's what the ghosts who haunt me now saw, or if they've ever felt like I've felt, somewhere between a god looking down on a battlefield and someone with no power at all, always torn between two rights or two wrongs. Before I knew it, the police were talking to my parents. When they showed up at the door, my dad immediately assumed it was for one of my brothers. Both my brothers are quiet, but the older one is so silent everyone thinks he must be running a whole criminal empire from his bedroom. The girl who I thought I was helping asked me not to say anything, and so I took it all, the doctors, the temporary exclusion from school, the flicked glances in my direction, the hushed tone I knew they used to speak about me, disgusted but with a kind of awe. Only my dad knew the whole story, and he tweaked my nose and said he was proud of me despite everything – concerned, of course, but a bit proud too. He told me I knew about duty, and that I was brave, even though I never thought I was. I'd told him the truth because I knew how worried he was, and didn't want him to think it was their fault, or that they'd gone wrong somewhere. I know I didn't calm him entirely, but I did a bit, and my father's pride is something I can hold on to, something I can fix my gaze on. But even so, January is still the worst of the months.

This January, I've dreamt about war every night for two weeks and the noise in my dreams, from men, horses and weapons crashing together, flattened into a single endless shriek, although I don't know which war it is. There are no clean wounds. People say now that I'm a violent girl, but apart from that one time my savagery is contained in the set of my shoulders and my refusal to smile in photographs. I try to follow the rules, but sometimes there are two rules that fight with each other, and so I fight with them. Sometimes right and wrong is decided afterwards. Sometimes the rules bend and don't make sense – if rules made sense, then ghosts wouldn't exist, but I know they do, because I've got three of them with me all the time, a girl and two boys, and they accompany me everywhere. I don't know why they chose to follow me. One of them, the girl, said once that it's because I understand both violence and rules, but I don't think that I do, only that I think that anger is a more honest thing than always giving in.

January, the worst month, the time the chill enters my bones and stays there, leaves rotting underfoot beneath ashtray-grey skies, a coward sun never daring to climb high enough in the sky to warm me. Everyone feels it; you can see it in the eyes downcast on the bus or sliding resolutely away from me, in faces lit only by glowing screens, ugly and green in untrue light. Every morning in January, even after nights when my dreams are less confused and cooler in feel, I get up when it is still dark and I go to the woods near our house to lay my face against cool bark. I see myself like a merciless giant compared to the mosses and creatures running their own miniature universe under the trees, only interested in me if I threaten them. I picture them building little shrines and making offerings to protect themselves from attacks, and I think of how if I trod on one of them it would seem malevolent and deliberate, when to me it would involve no thought at all. Gods do the same to little beetle humans on battlefields.

In my dreams about war there is one woman who calls herself Vengeance, and one who calls herself Justice, one named Duty and a nameless one who crouches above the walls of an ancient city I've never seen and howls for blood, barely a woman at all. I see a necklace wound around two pale hands, and I know with dream-certainty that this is the deadliest weapon of all. In the woods, I crouch down in the mulch and breathe in the frost and the smell of the earth, and imagine the mosses and beetles defying me with their lack of faith, and I close my eyes. I ask silently why, if I had to be haunted, it couldn't be by someone famous.

'We are famous,' says one of them, ferocious and interfering. I hadn't realised they could hear me when I didn't speak, so I resolve to stay quiet even in my thoughts, and instead stay hunched among the trees. That's what I did before the world turned up its grey blank light during this month, the worst month, the only month that is as bad as August.

They had arrived and glued themselves to my side last August, after the fight and all that happened afterwards. They never left, or rested, or said just what they wanted from me, only keeping up their speeches and their yelping, only talking to me of ideas that I had no interest in.

My parents and teachers and the doctor they sent me to all still speak constantly of their worries over my anger (although the doctor said 'troubled') and they would probably think it is significant, how the ghosts talk. They talk to me about blood, and justice, and how little a beetle human can do when faced with two duties of equal size, when the gods set them up to fail before they've even begun. Perhaps I had dreamed them too.

My daily visit to the woods began even before they arrived, and I would try to observe winter rolling over into spring when the dawn wasn't muddled by fog. I wanted to watch a pure light not yet dirtied by the day slice through the trees and pool golden on the ground at my feet. If only they would let me sleep, but the hours they keep are unpredictable.

****

Month 2: Hermaíos

I get the bus into school most days, and whenever I'm sad or tired I find the longest route I can, even if it's ages out of my way. My two older brothers have been rowing a lot lately, so I leave earlier and earlier – fierce quiet rows that set my teeth on edge and make my pulse echo too close to my lungs. I sit on one of my favourite seats (right-hand side window behind the buggy and wheelchair section on the bottom deck or right at the front on the top). I never end up listening to or reading anything, and instead look out at the city unfolding and resolving itself past the window. I like watching the other people too, seeing the way they hunch over their phones like soothsayers over a pond. I like their furrowed brows and silently moving lips. I know I must look like that myself.

My friends and I are usually in constant shapeless contact, no end and no beginning to conversations, the words like waves on a beach surging up and subsiding, but lately I've not been replying so much. As long as I send something once a day no-one will think I'm trying to attract attention by disappearing, and none of them have noticed my absence. I haven't told them about the unhappy transparent trio, the girl and her two brothers that no-one else seems to be able to see, or about my brothers fighting. I have to make space for them now on my bus rides. At first, I let them sit wherever they wanted, but once the girl sat on my lap and the mortal cold seeped right into my heart and lungs, and it took me days to warm back up.

My favourite time to ride the bus is February, because the passengers bring their chill on board with them, and together we fog up the windows. It's like we all share one breath, and I look around to see people shaking the day outside off their shoulders and settling down into their own silent column of air. It always spoils it for me when couples or groups of friends get on, who speak to each other and split the quiet.

If I time it right and take as odd a route as possible, I won't have my journey ruined by seeing someone I know. I like to think that everyone on the bus becomes one gently expanding and contracting organism, made up of different parts: old, young, disgruntled, like wet dogs in from a walk on a misty morning, shoulders straight and proud, wearing the cold late winter rain like jewels or medals on their coats. I rest my forehead on the cool grime of the bus window, just like I did in January with the trees, and think about how the three are here now, and I will never have to be alone.

****

Month 3: Prostatḗrios

I believed in ghosts when I was younger, but definitely wasn't afraid of them. People think I'm lying when I say this, but I rarely lie, whatever they might think of me. When I was six, I asked my mother what the tooth fairy did with all the teeth she took, and she told me that this was a fairy secret that we weren't allowed to know about. I asked if the tooth fairy lived in a place where you used teeth like money, and she looked troubled but said that no, it wasn't that, so when I wrote in a story that the tooth fairy had many houses built out of teeth, I don't think my teacher should have called an urgent meeting with my parents. I happily go into cemeteries and ruins, and the parts of London that ghosts are meant to like. Some of these are obvious, some less so. There are houses they're drawn to, and people, and particular trees.

One of the elephants in London Zoo has many spirit companions. They're all silent, but they sit with her and she doesn't seem to mind. There's a haunted bakery on Highgate Hill, and a park in Streatham with a phantom bandstand and ghost orchestra. They love tube stations and theatres, just like they're supposed to. The red brick house with the green leaves round the front door at the end of my street has played host to hundreds, although the three siblings are the first to live at my house. I ask them why they haven't gone there, and they become impatient and say that some other spirits might have been drawn to the red brick house, but they were drawn to me. I ask if they've ever glued onto anyone else in the way they have with me, and they seem puzzled by the question and say that they've lost count of how many there've been. They were from so long ago, and I've never heard of them when they tell me their names – Antigone, Eteocles, Polynices, (something that surprises and annoys them). Whenever I try to puzzle out what thread they've attached themselves to and travelled down like a zip wire to arrive at my side, it comes back to the same thing. An understanding of duty and obligation; fury both controlled and unleashed that they say shines off me in one powerful fog lamp beam. They'd visited and advised kings, queens, generals, war lords, philosophers. I am the first who's just been ordinary. They tell me that normally their chosen few have read about them at school. I ask what those people read about them, and if their story was anything like mine, but they keep stubbornly and unusually silent.

I ask them again why me, and they try to dismiss the question by saying it's only finite and limited beings like myself who are so obsessed with 'why'. They say reasons look different when you are eternal, but I ask again and again until at last they admit the trouble I'd been in attracted them, and that they saw something of their own experiences of injustice and conflict in me. Even so, in the great scheme, I am nothing special, and just one of a huge number of candle-flame lives that they have huddled round for warmth, that were then snuffed out by the great night. They are worn out from centuries of the same discussions and the same lack of resolution, and they are looking for someone new to join their gang, someone who might be able to offer a fresh perspective. A 'second pair of eyes', was what my dad would call it, although I am not sure that they do in fact have eyes, or if they had other phantom ways of seeing.

The eyes are the first to go when you die, one of the boys tells me but before I can ask more the girl shakes her head quickly, once, twice, so I shut up. Though they've sought me out, I feel as unimportant to them as the beetles in the woods are to me, as the dying soldiers outside the walls of Thebes were to the gods. I wonder if seeing time sped up is the key to wisdom and significance, if seeing emperors conquer and great cities built and crumble and thousands upon thousands of sunsets and sunrises lets them see the truth of things. When I ask them this, I cause more confusion. Time, the other boy says, hasn't sped up at all. Time has slowed to a dead stop. They go silent again when I tell them I now know the name of the place I dreamt about.

****

Month 4: Agriṓnios

Over Easter, me and my family go to Devon for a holiday, and the girl and her brothers come with us, although they shake their heads and seem baffled when I try to explain about the holiday, and how we will get chocolate eggs, and how my mum and dad will fight because my dad's mother will always want to be taken to church. I get impatient when they pretend not to understand that, because nobody has no problems at all with their families, even ghosts, and I think that with all their years of being tied to the earth they might have taken the trouble to learn the basic way the year is divided up in different places. All the way down in the car, they are in a strange mood, carrying on an argument that I thought they must have had on so many occasions before that none of them could remember the first time. I hadn't thought until now that ghosts could have moods – I think I'd assumed that to be present for so many hundreds of years would flatten their feelings into something more even and detached, but I am wrong. It is no longer an argument that can be won or resolved, but more of a performance, like a play, and their initial delight at my parents' car will not distract them or cheer them up for long.

Each of them has their part that they know so well that they can add their own little flourishes and what they want from me is nothing more than to be an audience, or at least that's what I'd thought at first. Creeping down the M4, my dad eyeballing other drivers who might be trying to sneak up the inside lane and force themselves in at the head of the traffic – he believes he can control bad behaviour with vigilance – I understand now that I have a part to play too. When the girl says that there is no stronger duty than that which one owes to one's family, I am meant to say that you also should be dutiful to your country. When she answers back that her family was a country, and worse yet, one that could never be repopulated after a disaster, I am supposed to respond by asking why her family could not rise from its own ashes.

I can have no more brothers than these, she says, suddenly losing interest in the discussion and her face closing up, losing the brightness that came from her enjoyment of the row and the performance. Cities can always have more sons. She turns away from me then, and leaves her brothers to continue the row, invoking funeral rites, just punishments, the rule of law, duty, duty, duty.

When we arrive in Devon, the sea glitters as if entertained by itself. I know how cold it will be, but still my sister and two brothers and I tear off our shoes and socks and run shrieking into the water, the cold gripping our ankles like iron. The unexpected spring sunshine makes little children of us again, and I feel, as I often do, a swell of love for them, and for my parents too. It gathers behind my nose like a sneeze. Perhaps because of the reputation I have now, people expect me to hate my brothers and sister, but I don't at all, although I believe the love I feel for them isn't returned. They treat me courteously, watchfully, like penguins at a zoo confronted suddenly with a heron. I don't love the girl and her brothers, but then I don't think they want me to. The girl and the two boys watch from the ridge up the beach, as old as some of the stones, and younger by centuries than some of the others. When you are cold like they are, the sea has nothing for you to fear.

****

Month 5: Homolő́ios

Exams are coming up, and my parents have turned into lunatics, bursting into my room unannounced at odd times – sometimes I think I understand the schedule and then they change things – taking my phone away, putting some blocker thing on my computer, threatening me with dire consequences if I do badly, and promising treats if I do well. I can get round the blocker and I know where they've hidden my phone and I can check it in secret a few times a day with my heart thudding about the idea of being caught, but I worry that they'll catch me talking to the three of them. It turns out that the ghosts find the concept of exams very funny. They keep hovering behind me and looking at my revision timetable and then retreating to the bed, laughing. I don't think I've ever seen them laugh before – smirk, yes, but they've never giggled so uncontrollably as they do when they discover 'historical sources'.

'Here is the only source you need,' says the girl. 'When one brother takes up arms against his family and his city, their sister's duty is cleaved in two, split from head to toe –.'

She always talks more than the other two. That is nothing strange to me since my sister keeps up a non-stop stream of burbling, bubbling observations from the moment she wakes up until she goes to bed at night. After that the words continue in silence, curled around her phone under the covers like a troll down in the caves greedily guarding a candle. My brothers barely speak at all, or raise their heads, or meet your eye, and when they fight with each other it's always sudden and quietly ferocious. This time though, maddened by revision and my parents' anxiety and knowing that there is definitely all kinds of stuff I'm missing because my parents have found a new hiding place for my phone, my violence comes rushing up my arms and neck. Even though I hardly respond to my real friends now all my time is taken up by the ghosts, I still want to see what everyone's up to, and I think about the notifications bursting onto the screen like tiny punctured hearts, and start shrieking at the three, 'What do you want from me, what's your unfinished business here, why won't you rest!'

They are shocked, you can tell, partly because they've never seen me behave like this and partly because they hadn't understood up until now how stupid I can be. There are no such things as unquiet spirits or spells and rituals to 'lay' them, they tell me. The ability to stay on earth and make common cause with the living, and to carry on learning new things after death is a gift only given to those either very great and powerful or very wicked. They won't answer when I ask which of these they are; they say eternal rest is something made up by envious beings glorifying their false god.

'We wouldn't have stayed if we hadn't wanted to,' says one of the boys. 'I missed my brother. I wanted to arrive at some understanding with him, before we went to the halls of death. I wanted to right some of the wrongs done by my parents and my parents' parents and their parents before that.' This is the longest speech he has ever made.

'You haven't learnt anything,' I say. 'You still get stuck in bus doors, although I don't know how, and you don't understand what a Bank Holiday is.'

The smiles they give me are pitying but edged with something bloodier. I throw a cushion at them.

****

Month 6: Theiloúthios

I can't really tell how the exams are going, but I enjoy seeing everyone who has been fooled by the people who were pretending to have done no revision, only to show up on the day looking crisp and focused with brand new clear pencil cases. The people who have been tricked look wild-haired and shell-shocked, as if this kind of treachery has never occurred to them. Treachery never does. The liars all stand about the halls waiting to go in, massaging their hands and fingers in a curious ritual. One of my mum's friends sent a video of how to do this to keep your fingers supple so they don't cramp up when you write. This woman had read somewhere that we'd lost the ability to write with pens, and our hands were frozen into screenclaws, and the video was posted in the mums' group chat. 'No wonder you can't hold a pen without your hand hurting', says the girl now, floating and looking at the people doing their hand ballet. 'When I was a girl we learnt great poems and could recite them on command. We were taught battle choreography. We were asked to think about the problems of life and death by our tutors. You, I've seen you, you can barely remember what you were going to buy from the market. I hope you're never asked to take up arms to defend your city, and you never have to defy your king.'

'Shut up,' I tell her, in my head. I've learnt to make use of the skill of talking to them without my lips moving and without anyone else knowing, since no matter what I try I can't keep my thoughts secret. 'Anyway, it's not even true. Learning long poems was a skill you had to spend years learning. Children didn't do it.'

'I am the last of the Royal House of Thebes, and my duty was heavy, yet I bore it bravely and did credit to my ancestors –'

I tune her out, and go into the exam hall where I produce an imperfectly remembered account of the root causes of the American Civil War. 'Blood, throne, honour, fate, that's what we used to fight battles over,' whispers one of the ghost brothers, reading my answers. I cover my writing up with my other hand.

****

Month 7: Hippodrómios

I think they're liars, those three. Their stories keep changing, whether or not they can touch objects, or if they can smell or taste or perceive colours. They say they don't need to eat, but I'm sure fruit's been going missing. I haven't eaten it, and neither have my brothers or sister, and there's only so many grapes my parents can munch through, hoping to set an example. They keep trying to start arguments with me about slavery, and about things they've seen in the news. The girl has become riveted by anything that she thinks of as injustice, and brings problems to me to solve. She seems to think I should share in her interests and obsessions because we're both girls.

'What do you mean, there's nothing you can do? I stood against plans for my execution by stoning, in order to carry out my sacred duty, I said my farewells to a man that loved me, and you cannot defy your rulers? Why not?'

I try to explain to her about how little power individuals have, and about elected representatives. I don't ask her more questions about whatever it was that had happened to her, mainly because I can tell she wants me to.

'Pah!' she says. 'This democracy of yours. Athenian rubbish! And how is it working, would you say?'

I can't and don't answer, because I am trying to choose what to wear to go out. Nothing looks right, and I've lost my best eyeliner. I ask her if she's seen it, and I see her hiding something behind her back. I give up, and push past her to get my bag. It must be me imagining things, but I'm sure I feel some solidity and resistance as I do so, when before I'd gone right through her as if she were a stream of ice-melt water.

'Why don't you know any of this? Aren't you supposed to have the wisdom of centuries? Do you learn things and just forget them?' I ask for the thousandth time.

'It has been many years since we last visited the living. We've been resting, and spending time only with each other,' she says at last. Even that doesn't seem true – either you are a wandering ghost or you aren't. 'Anyway, perhaps you are meant to be learning things from us. You don't know how to respond to a group of townspeople, or how to do penance for your family curses, or really anything at all.'

I ignore her.

'Where are you going?' she asks.

'Out,' I say.

'We're not coming. We're going to stay here and learn more things.'

If she is waiting for me to invite them along, she'll be waiting a long time.

'Good,' I say. 'I'm sick to death of you.'

Month 8: Pánamos

It's been a year now since they showed up. I'd never thought you could pick up ghosts in the summer rather than the darkness and gloom of winter, but that was when I'd first seen a hint of the girl, who had been the first one to appear, and even then, only just, and she disappeared if you tried to look at her directly. I'd started to worry I had a brain tumour or there was something wrong with my eyes, the way she shivered and darted at the corners of my vision, before finally appearing in the bathroom mirror behind me. My mother was working from home for August, and had shoved me out of the house in the morning saying 'you and your friends can stare at your phones together in the fresh air', and when I got home I was sunburnt and nauseous. That was when I saw the silvery-blue figure standing motionless and staring levelly just behind my right shoulder, watching me wash the smell of sunlit earth off my hands. Before the three of them, if I'd thought about it at all I would have described them as wintry shapes, not really people at all, which shows how little I know. They're much stronger now, and would never consider only appearing in reflective surfaces. They've emerged from behind the scenes now, that's for sure. No more looking mournfully out of the rippling surfaces of puddles, or sighing on the night winds that come in off the river.

Now it's the summer holidays again, the light comes early enough that when they wake me at the monk's hour with their questions and speeches, they could reasonably call it day, but the rest of the house dreams heavy under invisible fishing nets and can't hear them. They drive me out of the house and back to the woods, where I haven't been since winter. They settle down in the coppiced part, and give me expectant looks until I join them. One of the brothers shows me his wounds, which stand out more clearly in the dawn half-light. This is the time of the phantoms, and the siblings shimmer gently but somehow more substantially than usual in their little prayer circle, down here in the cathedral space described by the trees.

'For my treachery I was denied the proper rites, and left to be picked clean,' he says. His brother answers, 'when the war is done, and those picked clean and those honoured with a hero's funeral, do those men look any different from each other? Do the men whose women pour fragrant oils and sing laments, do they glow? Do the gods look on them with any greater favour?'

The wounded brother is quiet before admitting that no, they don't look any different.

'In that case, quiet your keening,' says his brother. 'Death is death.'

****

Month 9: Pamboiṓtios

Everyone's back at school now, and nobody wants to be the first to admit that they're relieved and that they'd felt the summer had gone on too long, but you can see it in their new clothes and haircuts, in revived skincare regimes and shiny bags. The ghosts have become interested in the haunted house at the end of the street, and go visiting there most days, and return with huge amounts of information. Their recall capacity makes me even angrier that they seem to retain so little of what I tell them, and still call any video they see a 'tiny play'. They ask where they might be able to learn more about the house and the other spirits who'd lived there, and to my surprise a memory leaps forward in an unwelcome blaze, as if it had been waiting for years to resurface and burn me, every detail sharp and unfaded.

I had been interested in the house myself, and had gone to the library to find out more about it (my parents say that the local library is a great and important resource, and we should use it gratefully before all the libraries are gone forever). I had asked the librarian, who was charmed by this kind of question from an eight-year-old, and had led me into a locked back room where she showed me a leather-bound volume with fragile brown pages that made a snapping sound when you turned them. In the volume were hundreds of accounts of sightings of ghosts at the haunted house on the corner of my street. Some of them were only a paragraph, and some were more like longer diary extracts, some spoke fondly of the spectral presence, some were frightened, some were angry, some involved religious men, some lived peaceably side by side with the ghosts, but it was hundreds of years' worth. They can't all have been lying.

I had thanked her, and then left, returning with my favourite notebook and asking if I could see the book again, and write down some of the stories I'd liked best. I had planned to use them for show-and-tell at school, but at the last minute I told my teacher that I hadn't brought anything when it was my turn, because I 'couldn't be bothered, Miss B'. I'd let the class's laughter die down before turning my grin to them, acknowledging my public. She went red in the face and asked for my parents to come in. I didn't want to say that I'd been afraid to share the contents of my notebook with the rest of the class, in case they formed the idea that I might be interested in something.

I tell the ghosts about the volume at the library, thinking they could probably pass through the locked door, and with a little prodding they get the story of show-and-tell out of me.

'You really are a coward, aren't you,' says one of the boys.

'Yes,' I say. 'I probably am.'

****

Month 10: Damátrios

I don't know when this happened, but they've started meeting up with other supernaturals. I thought that ghosts stayed in their little family groups, or were mainly solitary (although I knew that ghosts sometimes observed other bonds – crews of ships often stayed together, and so did dance partners and trade unions). Even so, I had assumed they kept themselves to themselves, and even though I didn't have much choice other than to believe in them now, I didn't think that anything else from the stories was real, but it turns out I am wrong.

One day mid-month one of the ghost brothers bursts through my bedroom door and starts telling me all about how he's met the tooth fairy, and how I've been wrong about her building houses made of teeth, when the truth is that she runs a small museum containing the treasures she takes. He describes the building, and is put out when I tell him that the cinderblock cube in the woods he is talking about is something to do with the electricity supply (I'm hazy on the details). He stands up very tall, and suddenly I can see how he must have looked in his armour, his eyes clear, his intentions grim but necessary.

'I met her,' he says. 'She runs a museum.'

Apparently, there are all kinds of things round here – spriggans, imps, sprites, goblins, even a vampire (although he's not very social, apparently, and prefers to keep to himself).

Our neighbours have put up this whole halloween display in the front garden, and the three are puzzled and disturbed by it. The bones of men are not decoration or jokes, says the girl and one of her brothers over and over. They should be given their proper and respectful burial.

'I never was,' says the other brother.

'You were, because I saw to it,' says the girl.

I explain that they aren't real skeletons, but plastic ones. This doesn't seem to reassure them, and their faces only clear when they ask if they could join me trick or treating (I think they have in mind to appear to other people and perhaps attract praise for how convincing their costumes are). I tell them that trick or treating is for babies, and their faces shut again. They tell me that they never stayed with one single person for as long as this, and now I won't agree to take them anywhere.

'You can go wherever you want! You're ghosts!' I say. They don't answer, but are moody with me for the rest of the week.

****

Month 11: Alalkoménios

Guy Fawkes is their new favourite story, and they ask to hear it again and again. 'He did what he thought was right, even though the punishment would be terrible. He obeyed the proper rules set out by his gods, and observed the proper rites,' says the girl.

'But what happens when that conflicts with what someone else thinks is right? Or if what you think is right results in people being hurt?' I ask, interested in the discussion in spite of myself.

The girl thinks about it for a moment and then says, 'If there is a conflict, then a battle is fought, and the victor says what was right all along. That's what happened to us. That's what happened to you.'

I agree to see the fireworks with my family as long as I can go out afterwards, which my parents reluctantly agree to, since my exam results a few months before had been better than any of us had expected. The three come with us, of course, although I tell them to keep quiet. They behave themselves, which is a surprise, since I really have nothing to threaten them with. They are enchanted by the fireworks, leaping and twinkling with every crackle and bang, and acting as if they've never seen anything like it, which they surely must have done. In the blue and purple flashes they appear more solid than ever. The edge of the woods pulses with all that lives here, and for a brief disoriented moment I think that the three of them are the gods after all, and I am nothing but a creature with no will of my own, and nothing else to do but wait and see what they have in mind for me. Perhaps it is nothing; perhaps if you live forever you lose interest even in your worshippers.

****

Month 12: Thiouios

My brothers have had a serious fight, the worst one they've ever had, and my oldest one has moved out and moved in with his girlfriend. My parents keep going into the front room with a bottle of wine and locking the door, emerging hours later with sore-looking red eyes. I'm back to visiting the woods, even though the damp and cold hangs in the air like patient jewels. The fight seems to have been brewing for decades, centuries even, and has blossomed up in one terrible explosion, lava bursting through a seam between grey rocks. My sister thinks I should pick a side, since our older brother is the one who left, but I don't want to do that. I'm not feeling festive, and know that we're not far away from January, the very worst month, the rotted leaf-scented month, the false hope of a new year when years mean nothing in these strange divisions set for us by people, and not gods.

'What does it mean, this December? If you spread your festivals throughout the year, you would give this month less power,' says the girl. 'You assign meaningless things such significance, and you ignore the meaningful. You will never have to choose between duty and death, because you have lost the concept of both.'

I tell her that if anyone has lost the meaning of death then surely it would have to be her and her brothers. By this time they have become truly solid. They could leave impressions in damp earth, they could float into shops and touch anything made of fabric (a new pastime of theirs), their flesh has stayed silver but with a milky opacity that shines pink and blue where the winter sun illuminates them.

'This is the beginning of the end,' she says. 'You're not happy here, and it's time for us to leave. Gather your courage, and come with us.'

I never had much courage in the first place. I decide to stay here.

REFLECTIONS ON THE STORY

While at university, I wrote my undergraduate dissertation on family curses in Greek myth, for which *Antigone* was one of the guiding texts. I was extremely pleased, then, when I was approached to write a story based on Sophocles' play. The pleasure soon turned to panic, however, when I realised how little of the play I remembered, so I tracked down my old copy in hope of inspiration. My previous engagement with the play had been in terms of considering how the play expressed the inescapability of fate and curses, and this was something I wanted to move away from. I also knew I didn't want to give a central role to the play's violence and misery, its grim backstory or equally grim conclusion, so I began to think about how I could connect its story and themes to the present day.

Re-reading it, I saw that the themes of competing loyalties, of injustice, state violence and familial duty seemed universal and timeless, but I also thought it would be interesting to cast the characters of the play's broader universe in the now, rather than to try to impose the themes on an entirely modern story. Additionally, thinking back to my earlier work on curses, I wondered about exploring the idea of eternal life, which could be seen either as a curse or a blessing (or a mixture of both) depending on the reader's perspective. The obvious choice, then, was to cast the characters as ghosts, and in my piece the ghosts of Antigone and her two brothers come across a young female narrator and select her for haunting. I decided to give my story a title taken from a line in one of M.R. James's ghost stories, in order to place it more firmly in that genre. Both of Antigone's brothers are already dead by the start of the play, so I took their descriptions and back stories from other plays about the same family, among them Aeschylus' *Seven Against Thebes*. While writing, I was mainly interested to see how far the themes could be universalised, and where the contrasts and conflicts might be between the experiences of young people from hugely different times and contexts.

In my story, the ghosts are far more interested in the modern world than the nameless narrator is in theirs – her preoccupation is far more personalised and particular: she is chiefly desperate to know why they have chosen her to haunt. She also has experienced unfair treatment by people in positions of power, which leads her to believe (rightly) that this is the thread connecting her to the ghosts. I was interested in thinking about how intention and meaning might be expressed in the context of immortality, and whether or not it is only the narrator, whose life is finite, who finds herself fixated on reasoning. The ghosts are far more aware of how the things that have affected them repeat themselves historically, and are keen for her to recognise their similarities. They are often frustrated by her failure to do so, just as she is frustrated by hearing them have what she feels to be the same conversations over and over. Antigone in particular is baffled by the narrator's unwillingness and inability to fight injustice in the wider world, even as the narrator tries to explain how little she as an individual can do. The narrator is a troubled and distressed young woman, who feels alienated from her friends and family, although she loves them, and often suffers from loneliness, even though she is not at all isolated. She comes to see, however, that she need not be defined by suffering or tormented by two sets of opposing duties and obligations, and in the end detaches herself both from the ghosts and from her fated connection to them. She realises that while there is value to be drawn from the ghosts of the past, and the ways in which their stories can help her find meaning in the present, it is not necessary to allow these spirits to shape or dictate her future.

Phoebe Roy

A Letter from Antigone

A poem by Barbara Bleiman

A Letter from Antigone

1943, Germany

Dear Sophie,
You were eleven when you and your friends
joined the League of German Girls,
while your brother, Hans, signed up for the Hitler Youth.
Sickened with what it was and what it said,
you almost didn't finish school.
Eleven years later, the guillotine fell
for treason against the state.
You'd joined the White Rose,
to argue against hate,
with words and papers fluttering down
like petals on the wind.
The scent of the white flower lingers still,
masking the crimson stench of your blood.

1955, Alabama

Dear Claudette,
You're fifteen and on your way home,
bussed to a school for students like you.
The seats at the front for white folks are full
but you stay sitting, with a woman, black like you,
bearing a child in her belly, black like you.
The police arrest you
and later you say,
'History kept me stuck to my seat.'
History is still glued to its seat
but people like you are trying to unstick it
to keep on sitting,
ask the reasons why
then stand up and make a better world.

1957, Arkansas

Dear Elizabeth,
There you are in black and white, holding a notebook
carrying the hopes of future girls like you,
cool in your sunglasses, calm in the faces
of anger around you, shouting
'Go back to Africa'.
You are fifteen and walk slow paces
into Little Rock Central High
to take your rightful place
in a school reserved for whites.
You look like it's just a normal day
though we know now,
for justice
you've just changed the world.

2008, Swat Valley

Dear Malala,
You are fifteen when a gunman stops the bus
and asks which one is you, then
shoots you straight in the face and through the neck.
You're fighting for the right to go to school
in Pakistan's Swat Valley, in your small town
where the Taliban have sent girls back,
saying female children must stay at home.
130 million girls cannot go to school
in countries across the world.
You got the education you wanted
and you have learned
to lead this fight for
every other girl to bravely board that bus.

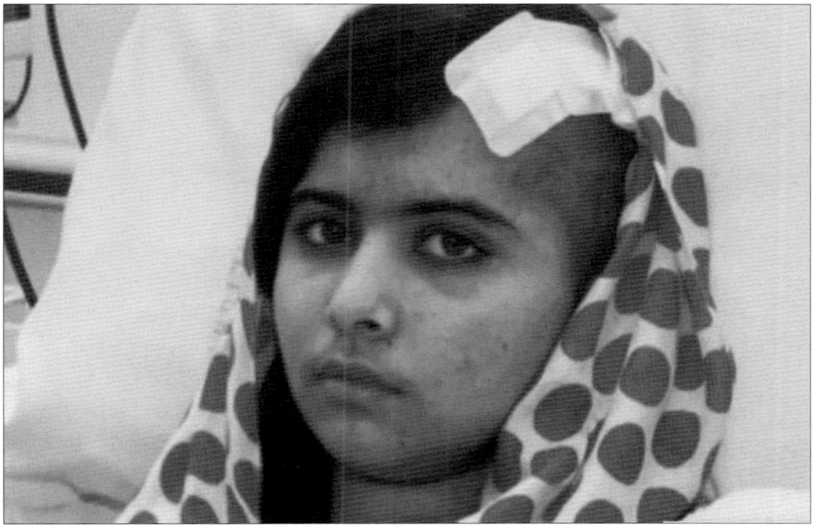

2018, Stockholm

Dear Greta,
You are fifteen when you stop going to school
and stand with a placard outside the Riksdag,
the Swedish parliament building.
Because of you, Fridays for Future begins,
with students striking every week and
frightened politicians suddenly
learning to listen to your voice.
Now, ducking and swerving the media crowd,
you make your own choices
with more on your mind
than who you're expected to be.
You're warning, joking, fighting
for people, for the planet, for you and me.

Antigone, in Ancient Times

Dear girls of the future,
I was your age when I stood up to power
against Creon, the new king.
He laid down the law and expected me to obey.
I needed to bury my brother,
to banish dishonour and an eternity without rest.
It was a crime to refuse.
The laws and rules are there for all of us –
they protect and provide –
but when they made no sense at all,
I did what I had to do.

Dear girls of the future,
who live in different worlds and times,
on journeys of your own
be happy and prosper, live and learn safely,
take up your own causes and
though it may be tough,
be brave.
Remember us,
who walked and sat and stood before.

Thinking of you,

Love Antigone

REFLECTIONS ON THE POEM

One of the things that struck me most forcibly when I read *Antigone* was the idea of a young girl speaking truth to power. Antigone is unafraid and uncompromising – she knows what she thinks is right and she holds firm, even when that brings great risk and ultimately death. Courage is the word that I'd use, a courage that most us ordinary people would probably like to show when faced with injustice but rarely do. So, when I came to write a poem based on the play, I thought about other girls and young women, throughout history, who have shown similar courage. Some are well-known, others less so. All had the same tenacity and certainty as Antigone, that there is something more important than their own lives, a need to stand up for what is right.

Barbara Bleiman

The Writers

BARBARA BLEIMAN

Barbara Bleiman is the author of two novels, *Off the Voortrekker Road* and *Accidents of Love*, and has recently published a collection of short stories, *Kremlinology of Kisses* (Blue Door Press). She has had several short stories published in *Mechanics' Institute Review, Shazkaz and Other Stories, Literary Shorts* and *Iridescent Adolescent*.

A recent collection of short stories for Young Adults, *An Inspector Called and Other Stories* is published by EMC. https://www.barbarableiman.com/

VALERIE BLOOM

Valerie Bloom MBE was born and grew up in Jamaica. She is the author of several volumes of poetry for adults and children, picture books, pre-teen and teenage novels and stories for children, and has edited a number of collections of poetry for children. She has presented poetry programmes for the BBC and has contributed to various radio and television programmes. She performs her poetry and runs writing workshops in schools, and conducts training courses for teachers worldwide.

Valerie won the 2022 CLiPPA – the CLPE poetry award – for her collection *Stars with Flaming Tails*.

https://valeriebloom.co.uk
Follow on Twitter @poetryval

INUA ELLAMS

Born in Nigeria, **Inua Ellams** is a writer and curator. He is a Complete Works poet alumnus and facilitates workshops in creative writing where he explores recurring themes in his work – identity, displacement and destiny – in accessible, enjoyable ways for participants of all ages and backgrounds.

His plays include *The Half-God of Rainfall*, *Black T-Shirt Collection*, *The 14th Tale*, *Barber Shop Chronicles* and *Three Sisters*. He founded The Midnight Run (an arts-filled, night-time, urban walking experience), the Rhythm and Poetry Party (The R.A.P Party) which celebrates poetry and hip hop, Film and Reel Mix, which celebrates film and interpretation and Poetry + Film/Hack (P+F/H) which celebrates poetry.

http://www.inuaellams.com/

SARAH HEHIR

Sarah Hehir is a poet and writer for radio, TV and the stage. Her writing for theatre is collaborative and experimental. She tells stories that focus on unheard voices and hidden stories. In 2013, she won the inaugural BBC Writer's Prize for her radio drama *Bang Up*, broadcast on BBC Radio 4 in 2014, and in 2016, her TV drama *The Seafort* was selected for the BBC TV Drama Writers' Programme. *Echoes Through the Dust* appears in *Short Plays with Great Roles for Women*. In 2016, *Zero Down* was transferred from Theatre 503 to The Pleasance, Edinburgh Fringe Festival. Sarah currently writes for BBC Radio 4's *The Archers* and BBC TV's *Doctors*.

She was born in Scunthorpe and now lives in the Medway Towns.

https://www.sarahhehir.com

PHOEBE ROY

Phoebe Roy is a writer and broadcaster from London. Her short story 'It Was Summer' won the Sceptre Loves prize in 2017, and in the same year her story 'Iridiscent Adolescent' was selected for inclusion in *A Change is Gonna Come*, an anthology of stories for young adults written by black and ethnic minority authors, which went on to win a special commendation in the Young Adult Book Prize. This story is the title story in the EMC anthology *Iridescent Adolescent*. She is currently working on her first novel.

Workshopping The Facility

Year 10 students at Rochester Grammar School take part in a workshop on The Facility

In these photos the students explore the role of the Chorus.